KIDS MENTORING KIDS

Making a Difference

a guide for students to help others
achieve their highest potential

GAIL A. CASSIDY

BALBOA.PRESS
A DIVISION OF HAY HOUSE

Balboa Press books may be ordered through booksellers or by contacting:

Balboa Press
A Division of Hay House
1663 Liberty Drive
Bloomington, IN 47403
www.balboapress.com
1 (877) 407-4847

ISBN: 978-1-9822-4838-3 (sc)
ISBN: 978-1-9822-4839-0 (e)

Print information available on the last page.

Balboa Press rev. date: 06/16/2020

ACKNOWLEDGEMENTS

Tom, Lynne, and Tommy--you are my foundation, my life, my motivation. I am blessed to have your love. You will always have mine. I am especially appreciative of my daughter-in-law, Elizabeth, and my extra special grandsons, Patrick and Jason! What a joy to have you all in my life!

To write a book requires a writer to have a strong belief in the importance of getting a particular message out to the public. My message is simple. Everyone is special in some way, and when a person is able to recognize and act on that something special, the world benefits. Being a mentor allows that to happen.

This book is dedicated to my Union County Vocational/Technical Adult School students and my Roselle Catholic students. I learned more from you than you ever could have learned from me. Thanks for the lessons.

Thank you, thank you, thank you all!

CONTENTS

PART - 1   THE IMPORTANCE OF MENTORING   1

    Mission Statement   3
    Foreword   4
    Welcome   6
    The Importance of Mentoring   8
    Rationale for Mentoring   10
    The Best Solution: Mentoring   12
    Overall Goals for Mentorees: To Achieve   14
    Mentoring Workshop Overview   15

PART - 2   PEOPLE SKILLS   19

    Overview of Part Two   21
    Self-Esteem and Values   22
    S-A-V-E   28
    The Philosophy of Kids Mentoring Kids Consists of Five Specific Provisions: 34
    The Mentor's Code of Ethics   35
    Communication Skills   57
    Communication Problems   58
    Body Language   59
    Body Language Cues   63
    Try to Understand Before You are Understood   67
    Human Relation Skills   69
    Review of Section Two   71

PART - 3   ESSENTIAL SKILLS: 73

    Overview of Part Three   75
    Effective Questioning Techniques   76
    The Mentor's Communication Secret Listening   78
    Tolerations   83
    The Importance of Belief   85

PART - 4   MENTOR TRAINING   **89**

    Overview of Part Four   91
    Worksheet for Mentorees   92
    Mentor Preparation   93
    Mentoring Preparation Form   95
    How to Prepare for Your Mentoring Session   96
    Assessment   98
    S.M.A.R.T. Goals   100
    10 Goals to Reach in the Next 90 Days   102
    Things to Talk About   103
    Additional Suggestions for Meetings   108
    Questions to Ask when Conversation Slows Down   109
    Challenges for Your Mentoree: 112
    Mentor Awareness   113
    7 Habits of Highly Ineffective Mentors   115
    Miscellaneous   116
    Review   117

PART - 5   PRACTICE SESSIONS   **119**

    Case Studies   121
    Review   126

PART - 6   MENTORING PROGRAM ORIGINS   **129**

    Overview of Part Five   131
    Mentor Program Origins   132
    References   139
    Works Cited and Consulted   141

APPENDIX A   **143**

    Two Additional Courses to Ensure Acceptance and Validation   145

APPENDIX B   **155**

    Tips on How to be the Best that You Can Be   157

PART ONE

THE
IMPORTANCE
OF
MENTORING

MISSION STATEMENT

MISSION OF MENTORING LEADERSHIP TRAINING

The mission of the Mentoring Leadership Training Workshop is to train students with the capability for ethical leadership and self-actualization both independently and as members of a community.

GOAL

The goal of Mentor Training Workshop is to provide students with the tools necessary to participate to their fullest in and outside of the school community.

MAJOR BENEFITS FOR THE SCHOOL

Reduced incidents of bullying, improved individual self-concepts, and higher graduation rates.

INDIVIDUAL MENTOREE BENEFITS

Enhanced self-concept, acceptance, validation, self-actualization.

Gail A. Cassidy

FOREWORD

FOR TEACHERS

Two-time Academy Award winning actor, Denzel Washington, attributes his success to his childhood mentor. As he says, "You don't go it alone." In his book, *A Hand to Guide Me*, Washington states, "We're all meant to walk a certain path at a certain direction for a certain purpose." He then tells the stories of over sixty well-known people who attribute their success to some form of a mentor, i.e., coach, teacher, family member, priest, rabbi, friend, etc.

Mentors can also be found among peers. *Kids Mentoring Kids* helps younger teens who may be having difficulty in school, either with their classes or with their peers or something outside of school, by assigning them to a student in a higher grade.

Working with an upperclassman who has been trained in a variety of skills: mentoring skills, communication skills (including body language, voice, and words), human relations, effective listening, questioning techniques, is an invaluable experience for the younger student.

Kids helping kids provides growth for both the mentor and the student being mentored. The goal is to provide teens with the tools necessary to participate to their fullest inside and outside the school community.

Mentoring younger students is a huge and rewarding undertaking for students. All students, mentors and mentorees, benefit from this program. As humanitarian Albert Schweitzer said, "Every person I have known who has truly been happy has learned to serve others." This is an opportunity for students to help others.

Although the program was initially designed for students who needed help, whether academically or socially, it was the mentors also also benefitted from the mentoring experience. Students of all ages want to feel accepted and validated. Those desires are fulfilled by their mentor.

Statements from the mentors at the end of the year showed they benefitted as much as their mentorees. "I felt important." "It was the first time I felt looked up to." "I like the fact that I can be trusted and that I can help someone else." "I know that I need someone to talk to sometimes—being there for someone else is great." "I've learned that I can be a bigger person, a person to go to in a time of trouble," and "I loved helping the underclassmen" were typical of the responses from the mentors on follow-up of the programs.

The responses from parents of those being mentored were also positive. A typical response is from one mother who said her son actually looks forward to going to school. Before that, he was scared to leave his home. Teachers commented on improved grades of those being mentored.

The major benefits of *Kids Mentoring Kids* are reduced incidents of bullying, improved individual self-concepts, improved grades, and improved attitudes. When a child realizes his potential, he has a much greater probability of reaching it. Mentors make a difference!

The primary goals for both mentor and mentoree include enhanced self-esteem, acceptance, validation, and self-actualization. Teens learn how they can be the best that they can be and teach their mentorees the same.

Mentoring younger students is a huge and rewarding undertaking for your students. In order for them to not only learn the material but also appreciate its importance, small group discussions are encouraged throughout the program.

Listening to their concerns will provide you with invaluable feedback.

There are no wrong responses, only honest, heartfelt concern; and those concerns need to be addressed.

Students are asked to keep their own personal Journal in which they will be asked to respond to different segments of the program. After they have written in their Journals would be is a good time to hold class or small group **DISCUSSIONS** on what they have written.

Assignments for students will appear in boxes throughout the program.

All students, both mentors and mentorees, benefit from this program.

As you, the teacher, serve your students, your students will now learn how to serve others.

The Course is divided into seven segments: (1) Importance of Mentoring, (2) People Skills, (3) Essential Skills (Questioning, Listening, Tolerations, Belief), (4) Mentor Training Techniques, (5) Mentor Training Origins, (6) Practice Sessions, (Appendix A) - Additional Courses, (Appendix B) - Tips Booklet on How to Be the Best That You Can Be.

Videos on teaching this course can be purchased at https://www.cassidycourses.com.

WELCOME

Dear New Mentor,

Welcome to your class on mentoring. That you are involved with this program speaks volumes about you, the loudest being your concern for others, in this case younger students. Some underclassmen may be having challenges with some aspect of school. The problems could be with friends, teachers, or classes. They may experience fear, anxiety, or even bullying—whatever it is that's making school a less-than-stellar experience for them.

I am delighted that you have chosen to take this course, a clear indication that you are interested in helping others. You may have experienced challenges some time in your life, and you want to prevent others from experiencing the same. You may just desire the good feeling that comes with making a difference in the lives of others. Whatever reason you have for wanting to become a mentor, I applaud your decision. Helping others not only feels good; it also changes lives.

The information in this book works equally as well with friends, family, or anyone who desires to improve his life, change her job or just get things done. Everyone can use a mentor. Everyone wants to improve in some way.

ASSIGNMENT: Take a moment to think, then write in your Journal, about something that has happened in your earlier school days when you would have appreciated someone to talk to, someone to understand what you were feeling.

BACKGROUND

Seeing kids picking on other kids, i.e., bullying them, has always been something that made me hurt for the child being hurt, and this is where the positive effect a mentor has on another person is so important, and this is where you come in—someone who can help someone else!

> When I was five years old, I experienced a specific event that that not only made a lasting impression on me but also awakened my awareness of the existence of bullies, people who prey on those whom they consider weak, defenseless, or "less than" they are. I particularly remember the feeling of helplessness that I experienced that day. That I can so clearly recall this event today signifies the impact it had on my life.
>
> As a young child I watched bullies repeatedly pick on my brother because he was not a strong boy. He had been born with a heart problem.
>
> One day when I was five and he was seven, we were playing together when a group of boys picked up rocks from the nearby train tracks, taunted us, and then started pelting us in the backyard of our row house. We were trapped. The metal cellar door had latched

when we came out, and we would have had to walk ten houses toward the tracks, closer to the bullies, in order to get to the front of the houses. We didn't have time.

One rock hit my brother in the temple. He collapsed to the ground and lay motionless. I remember screaming until my mother heard me and ran out, found my brother, carried him inside and called the doctor. (In those days the doctor came to the house.) There lay this seemingly lifeless form on our living room sofa, and I was terrified that my nearest and dearest friend was dead.

He regained consciousness and fully recovered, but that attack was the earliest event that I can remember which served as a catalyst to create my passion to help and protect others, especially young people who are not as strong as their peers, who perhaps have not had the good fortune to be born into a "comfortable" home, who have not been schooled adequately for whatever reason, who do not speak English as their first language, who have not experienced acceptance by her peers and/or adults, who may or may not have graduated from high school and/or college.

These are the younger students who need your help. Many may be potential dropouts, young people who must learn to take 100% responsibility for all of their actions and who need your guidance to do so. Nobody gets through life without help. Everyone needs support and validation. Young people need help in every stage of their development, and your assistance will make a difference in their lives.

Many younger students may honestly wonder if they can change. "Assume a virtue, if you have it not" is the advice Shakespeare would have given them. In other words, pretend to be strong or happy or positive, and you will become so. Fake it until you make it.

Students need to be encouraged to start acting as they desire to be, and they need to know they can be whatever they desire, one step at a time. The capacity for creating the life they want resides within each of them.

Being a mentor means showing acceptance and guidance to someone who needs your support. Your reward is the tremendous satisfaction awaiting you as you watch your mentorees grow and develop into the people they desire to be.

In essence, you will be a coach, counselor, guide who seeks, finds, and points out the strengths of his mentoree. This implies recognition of someone's strengths, and everyone has them.

I hope you enjoy your new role as mentor.

Enjoy the course,
Gail Cassidy

ASSIGNMENT: In your Journals, write any time(s) that you can recall when you would have liked to have someone to talk to about a problem you were experiencing. If you have ever been bullied, write about your experience, how you felt and how you reacted.

THE IMPORTANCE OF MENTORING

The primary objective of this course is not only to explain to you exactly what you'll be doing, i.e., mentoring, but also why it's so important not only for your mentoree and also for the knowledge and understanding that you will come away with.

One famous actor you may be familiar with, Denzel Washington, believes that his success in life is due to a mentor he had as a teenager in an after--school boys' club.

He was born and raised in a relatively poor part of New York. The streets were tough, and gangs were prevalent. Had Denzel taken the wrong path, he certainly would not be the famous Denzel Washington we know, the person who has gained fame through his movies and through his acts of kindness.

He wrote a book called *A Hand to Guide Me*. His book showcases how mentors shape the lives of people we all know and respect, from baseball legend Hank Aaron, Mohammed Ali, Bob Woodward (Bob Woodward who was a reporter during the Nixon era). The names Yogi Berra, Danny Glover, the actor, Whoopi Goldberg, and over 60 famous people are well recognized. Each person he wrote about had a mentor, somebody who believed in them and encouraged them on their paths to success.

Most people have had a mentor at some point in their lives. He or she may have come in the form of a teacher, a parent, a relative, an aunt, uncle, maybe a guardian, an older friend, a counselor, a coach, a minister, priest, rabbi, tutor—somebody who believed in them, encouraged them to be the best they can be, and someone who had a positive influence on them.

It's amazing how having somebody believe in you really makes you want to do the best that you can do. Sometimes people around us—our parents or people who are close to us—are just too busy surviving, earning a living; and that's where you come in. That is exactly what you'll be doing—accepting and encouraging your mentoree to be the best that he or she can be.

You now have an opportunity to impact your mentoree's life. Think about who it is in your life who has encouraged you. Keep thinking about that during the week.

ASSIGNMENT: In your Journal, reflect on the people in your life who have made a difference? Who is the person or persons who believe in you and have encouraged you?

THOUGHTS TO PONDER
"Why Be a Mentor?"

- To *mentor* means to assist a *valued mentoree* move from where he or she is to where he or she wants to go. -Unknown
- Mentoring is about two people, talking together and learning from each other. -Kaplan/Newsweek guide on "How to Be a GREAT MENTOR."

- *In his State of the Union Address, President Bush said,* "Government will support the training and recruiting of mentors, yet it is the men and women of America who will fill the need. One mentor, one person, can change a life forever--and I urge you to be that one person."
- A research study provided these results on mentoring. "Children who met with a mentor three times a month for one year were 46 percent less likely to begin using illegal drugs, 27 percent decrease in initiating alcohol use, 37 percent decrease in lying to parents, 52 percent less likely to skip school, and 33 percent less likely to get into fights." (Statistics from a nationwide review of Big Brother/Big Sister's Programs by Tierney & Grossman)
- Why has mentoring grown into a social movement supported by government, schools, businesses and religious institutions alike? Because it works.
- Recognize that a mentor is a caring and concerned person. A mentor is a listener and a guide. That's the role you will be playing.

(In order to simplify reading, the author has chosen to switch between the use of male and female pronouns rather than constantly writing him/her.)

Gail A. Cassidy

RATIONALE FOR MENTORING

Maslow's Hierarchy of Needs is a frequently used method to describe the stages of people's development. Developed by psychologist Abraham Maslow in the early1940s, this theory contends that as humans strive to meet their most basic requirements, they also seek to satisfy a higher set of needs.

Maslow presents this set of needs as a hierarchy, consisting of:

1. **(Survival)** - Physiological/bodily
2. **(Security)** - Safety needs
3. **(Social Acceptance)** - Love/belonging needs
4. **(Self-Esteem)** - Ego Status
5. **(Making a Difference)** - Self-actualization— the desire to be "all that you can be."

This theory contends that the most fundamental level of existence starts with **Survival**, the physiological need for food, water and shelter.

Once that requirement is fulfilled, **Security** becomes paramount. Maslow believed that the higher-level needs, such as **Social Acceptance** and **Self-esteem**, could only be met after the lower level ones had been satisfied.

Most mentorees have the basic elements of the first two steps in their lives in one degree or another; however, a few of your mentorees may not be experiencing safety and security. Their homes may be danger zones because of family discord or their homes may be in a dangerous location. One time when they can be assured of "safety"-- mental and emotional--is during their meetings with their mentors.

In order to maximize their potential, *mentorees first must feel they are safe, accepted, and respected as they are.* What helps to instill this feeling is constantly seeing the invisible tattoo on their foreheads, which reads, "Please make me feel important." In other words, "Don't criticize me or make me feel like a loser."

As a mentor, it is your job to help your mentorees move through phase three, ***Social Acceptance*** and phase four, ***Self-Esteem***, in order to facilitate their reaching the highest level, five, ***Self-Actualization***. This final phase puts your mentoree in a position to make a difference in the world.

Feeling important in some way is one of the deepest needs all human beings desire to have fulfilled. The words imply *acceptance*, and they imply *capability*, which is the basis of Level Three on the Hierarchy, "***Belongingness or Social Acceptance***." *Everyone wants to be accepted,* either by their peers, family, church choir, neighborhood friends, teachers, or whoever is important to them in their lives.

It has been said that "There is more hunger for love and appreciation in this world than there is for food."

Once the feelings of acceptance occur, mentorees can reach toward the next Level, *"Esteem/Ego Status."* You, as their mentor, facilitate movement from one level to another, as you will see in the *Mentoring Code of Ethics.*

In one way or another, people young and old will gravitate toward someone who provides a source of validation. Validation is a human need, and this is where being a mentor comes into play. This is your opportunity to help mentorees experience both acceptance and validation.

The fifth level of the Hierarchy is ***Making a Difference***. With the help of mentors, mentorees could reach the point where they can make a difference--in their own lives and in the lives of those for whom they care.

It is important to remember that *positives do work*. If mentorees believe they can improve, they will. George Reeves, sixth grade teacher of Norman Vincent Peale told his special student, "You can if you think you can." And Peale proved his teacher right.

Overcoming years of negativity and poor results may be the greatest challenge for those who are unmotivated. While your mentoree's improvement may not be vast, their improvement is possible by moving in small increments toward a higher level of proficiency in their job skills and their interpersonal skills.

ASSIGNMENT: In your Journal, write the level you are on in Maslow's Hierarchy of Needs and explain why.

MENTOR HINTS

- Authenticity and self-expression are core qualities in a mentor and leader.
- Remember that it is not personal. Sometimes you are the only person they trust to see them as they are behind the facade.
- Mentors do not have all the answers.
- Give mentorees their wings and encourage independence.
- The most valuable gifts you can give the youth are time, support, and faith in their abilities.
- Encourage healthy risks and provide opportunities to excel.
- Understand them and encourage them to change negative behaviors. Some youth start off as negative leaders. They need to be seen for what their potential is.
- Everyone has inner strength and something positive to contribute.

THE BEST SOLUTION: MENTORING

Picture yourself awakening each morning without an alarm clock, with a smile on your face, and a feeling of excitement in your stomach, ready for what the day may bring. When you work at what is truly meaningful to you and when you have a real purpose in life, you will wake up each morning excited and happy about the day that is about to unfold.

You now have the opportunity to work with a mentor, someone who understands what you have gone through and where you are right now.

A mentor will help a mentoree reach their goals so they can feel excited and happy with what they are doing. All that a mentoree has to do is complete the Mentoring Preparation Form each week and meet with their mentor.

TOP 15 BENEFITS OF WORKING WITH A MENTOR

1. Mentors become familiar with their mentoree, their background, interests, and goals.
2. Mentors can help mentorees discover dreams and activities that made them feel special.
3. Mentors can help mentorees to find their life's purpose.
4. Mentors can help mentorees prepare to earn a good living wage.
5. Mentors can help mentoree find greater happiness in their lives.
6. Mentors can help mentoree learn how to come to terms with their past.
7. Mentors can help mentoree restore their energy.
8. Mentors can help mentoree get their needs met.
9. Mentors can help mentoree capitalize on their skills and abilities.
10. Mentors can help mentoree live by their value system.
11. Mentors can help mentoree eliminate things in their lives that are not in their best interests.
12. Mentors can help mentoree maintain an upbeat, positive attitude.
13. Mentors can help mentoree handle difficult, challenging situations.
14. Mentors can help mentoree develop a stronger community.
15. Mentors can help mentoree be the best person they can be.

You, the student mentor, are the key to getting and holding their attention.

Mentoring does enhance a student's feelings of success by enabling them to experience validation and acceptance, from someone they respect. What is foremost in the minds of most young people is their quest for identity and their attempt to develop some sense of personal power.

When you, as a mentor, recognize these needs, you can help fulfill their desire by introducing them to mentoring, a method of coaching which promotes equality, fairness, justice, respect--qualities that are important in everyone's life. This method enables each mentoree to enjoy confidence, acceptance, growth, and an appreciation of his or her imagination, all essential elements of self-esteem.

BENEFITS

Benefits abound from student mentoring. Responses from the mentor are sincere. Values are finally understood by the way they are discussed and considered. The mentor's words display their respect for what the mentoree knows and feels. By talking in terms of possibilities, rather than certainties, mentors come to understand that the way they speak, as much as what they say, has real consequences. Mentorees look up to mentors because they can relate to someone close to their own age.

EXPECTATIONS

Mentorees need to know what is expected of them. This cannot be taken for granted, Reading teacher, Janet Allen (*It's Never Too Late: Leading Adolescents to Lifelong Literacy*), surveyed one of her classes where she found that 51.65% of the students had no idea how to become better readers. 17.58% believed the answer was good books. Other responses included 14.29% "read to me," 13.19% "make me read," and 3.30% "read a lot" (46). The point is mentors need to set expectations for their mentors as well as provide them with answers when they can do so.

In business, managers have expectations of their employees, and frequently the employees do not know what those expectations are. To do a good job, a person has to know what is expected for him to do and/or accomplish and how to do it.

It is the mentor's responsibility to work together with her mentoree so she will know what steps need to be taken to go to the next level. The Mentoring Preparation Form will serve to keep mentorees on track.

The point is simple. People respond to what is expected of them. In order to be successful in response, the person has to know how to fulfill the expectation(s). As a mentor, you can help your mentoree find her way by showing the way.

OVERALL GOALS FOR MENTOREES: To Achieve their highest potential according to their aptitudes and dreams.

1. To encourage mentorees to find their own answers (discourage dependency) and solve their own problems. (Mentors give guidance, not answers).
2. To have mentorees identify steps needed to improve different areas of their lives. (See Assessment).
3. To establish self-reliance and trust.
4. To be supportive and accepting.

Before covering the "how to" of holding mentoring sessions, first look at the next two pages, the double-sided Placemat, that covers the basics every mentor should be aware of when interacting with mentorees.

MENTORING WORKSHOP OVERVIEW

The next two pages, **THE PLACEMAT SUMMARIES,** are summaries of everything we will be covering in this Mentoring Leadership Workshop.

We have already covered:

The Importance of Mentoring
Rationale for Mentoring
The Best Solution: Mentoring
Workshop Overview

The next two pages can be copied and put back-to-back similar to a placemat and can be used at mentoring sessions as a reminder of what you need to cover and questions you can ask. A plastic page-holder is recommended to keep the pages together and in good condition.

The Mentoring Leadership Training Workshop

"It is okay to be me--the best me I can be!"

MISSION: The mission of the Mentoring Leadership Training Workshop is to train students with the capability for ethical leadership and self-actualization both independently and as members of a community.

GOAL: The goal of Mentor Training Workshop is to provide students with the tools necessary to participate to their fullest in and outside of the school community.

MAJOR BENEFITS FOR THE SCHOOL: Reduced incidents of bullying, improved individual self-concepts, and higher graduation rates.

INDIVIDUAL BENEFITS: Enhanced self-concept, acceptance, validation, self-actualization.

AMBIANCE FOR ALL MEETINGS

S - A - V - E

S - SAFE
A - ACCEPTANCE
V - VALIDATION
E - ENTHUSIASM

THE MENTORING CODE OF ETHICS

THE BAKER'S DOZEN

General Guidelines for Working With Your Mentorees

1. **SHOW RESPECT TO GET RESPECT**

   Know that your friends "mirror" you.
   They reflect what they see,
   hear, and feel from you.

2. **BE NONJUDGMENTAL**

   Accept your classmates as they are, and provide the atmosphere for them to grow in a positive manner.

3. **SEEK THE STRENGTHS OF YOUR CLASSMATES**

   - Help your peers to recognize their specialness.
   - Remember that everyone desperately wants to feel special.
   - See the invisible tattoo on every student's forehead that reads: "PLEASE MAKE ME FEEL IMPORTANT."

4. **PROVIDE A SAFE ATMOSPHERE**

5. **KNOW, YOU cannot NOT COMMUNICATE**

6. **SET HIGH EXPECTATIONS**

   Remember the story of a new teacher who thought the locker list from 140-160 was the list of IQ's in her class and she treated them accordingly, and they performed accordingly.

7. **MAKE SINCERITY YOUR NUMBER ONE PRIORITY**

8. **BE SENSITIVE**

9. **SET BOUNDARIES**

10. **HAVE FUN!**

11. **SMILE:** It warms a room.

12. **BE (OR ACT) ENTHUSIASTIC** about everything you do.

    It's contagious.

13. Remember, **PEOPLE HAVE TWO BASIC NEEDS:**

    1) TO KNOW THAT THEY ARE LOVABLE and 2) THAT THEY ARE WORTHWHILE.

---

copyright Gail Cassidy

Primary Goal of Mentoring Leadership Workshop:

**To achieve each student's highest ethical leadership potential
according to his or her aptitudes and dreams.**

Your beliefs guide you. If you think you can or you think you can't, you are right.

Confidentiality EXCEPT if you become aware of

- Physical, sexual, or emotional abuse
- Suicide possibility
- Illegal weapons
- Substance Abuse
- Danger to self or others

QUESTIONING

- **Ask question**
- **Paraphrase**
- **Pause**
- **Question**

Listening

- Be silent
- Hear words spoken and not spoken
- Listen with senses
- Reflect back what you hear
- Ask for further clarification
- Prompts

Listen for

- Authenticity and Truth (tone & language)
- True desires
- Fears
- Support
- Positives
- Your reactions to mentoree

Non-Verbal Communication You Cannot NOT Communicate

55% - What you SEE
38% - What you HEAR
7% - Words used

Preparation Form

- What accomplished since last session?
- What didn't get done, but intended to?
- Challenges and problems?
- Opportunities available now?
- What I want to work on today?
- What I promise to do by next meeting.

Human Relation Skills

- Accept people as they are.
- Be enthusiastic in all you do.
- Listen. It is the greatest compliment you can pay someone.
- Thoughts. Change your thoughts and you change your world.
- You can't control what happens to you, but you can always control your reactions.
- Accept what is, e.g., Serenity Prayer.
- Treat others as you wish to be treated.
- Do not criticize other people. No one ever appreciates it.
- **Look for the positives in everyone.**

Things to Talk About

- **How are you feeling about yourself?**
- **How are you looking at your life?**
- **How are you feeling about others?**
- **What has occurred since our last meeting?**
- **Any breakthroughs or insights?**
- **New choices or decisions made?**
- **Personal news?**

More Talking Points

- **Progress on goals, projects, activities?**
- **What have you done that you're proud of?**
- **What resistance are you encountering?**
- **Can I explain something for you?**
- **Can I provide you with more information?**
- **Do you need help developing a plan?**
- **May I offer you a strategy or advice?**
- **What is your next goal or project?**

"Wants"

- **Where do you want to live, work, school?**
- **How do you want to look, feel, sound?**
- **What do you want to do every day?**
- **Desired relationships with family, friends?**
- **What obstacles do you see keeping you from doing what you want in life?**
- **How can I help you succeed?**

Interests

- What do you feel strongly about? News that upsets you on TV?
- Whom do you admire and why?
- Where do you enjoy being?
- What do you do in your spare time?

Gail A. Cassidy

PART TWO

PEOPLE SKILLS

OVERVIEW OF PART TWO

Effective mentors need to understand the basics of Human Nature. This knowledge helps not only the mentoree but also the mentor.

NO. #1 RECOMMENDATION: Keep a Journal and complete the assignments in each section. At the end of the course, your completed Journal will reveal what you have learned about yourself as well as what you have learned about your mentoree.

Before the basics of the Mentoring Process are covered, you will cover the following:

- Self-Esteem and Values
- S-A-V-E, an acronym for positive human interactions
- The Philosophy of Kids Mentoring Kids
- Code of Ethics (told from a retired teacher's point of view)
- Communication Skills: Body language, Voice, Words
- Human Relation Skills
- Review of Section Two

SELF-ESTEEM AND VALUES

The Background of How Kids Mentoring Kids Began

We become what we envision. -Claude Bristol

One-on-one mentoring began after I became aware of the impact students' stories had on their classmates. Having a mentor to talk to allows the mentoree to feel free to discuss potentially uncomfortable subjects.

The writing class described below was the motivation to start Kids Mentoring Kids.

Mentoring has a positive effect on a mentoree's self-esteem and values. The values of mentorees are frequently uncovered through the act of meeting and talking each week.

Listening is the greatest compliment we can pay another person, especially one who has not experienced being valued. By listening to their stories, mentors will hear their mentorees' personal values revealed.

Without conscious awareness of their values, mentorees frequently reveal them through their choice of topic and through their method of handling the topic. For example, two young ladies spoke out strongly against abortion, but the ensuing discussion revealed that they were speaking out against teenage sex and the resultant lack of responsibility on the part of teens.

"Any system of values should be scrutinized in terms of its consequences for human life" (Louise Rosenblatt, *Literature as Expectation*). Because of the history of "at risk" students, instructors and mentors should listen closely to determine the values, which determine the action of the mentorees. Unfortunately, I learned that some teenagers value "coolness" over health and safety as evidenced by the story one student wrote.

> I have repeatedly told my best friend, "Do not get your tongue repierced!" Here is how it starts. She got her tongue pierced on Saturday, and a mutual friend of ours and I told her that the earring in the tongue looked too crooked and that it just did not look right. She insisted that it was all right. She slept with it that night, and when she woke up the next morning, she had blood all on her bedding.
>
> She still did not think much of it. She later on that day went out and found someone at a body-piercing parlor who told her that the bar in her tongue was crooked; and when they pierced it, they came very close to piercing the main vein in the tongue. She then had to take out the bar, so she only had the earring for about 24 hours. She has been told by many kids in the school to go see a doctor, that she should not mess around with that, but she thinks that nothing is wrong, that it is fine.

She cannot really complain too much because she did not tell her mom, and if her mother found out, she would kill her. She thinks that she is invulnerable to getting an infection, so here is my advice to her. I said, "Do you really want this that bad that you will go through so much pain to have a stupid earring in your tongue?" I also told her that it is not worth it. When her parents find out they will be very upset, and that is really not worth it.

I got the same response from her that her parents would get from her. I told her that I know a lot of people that have gotten their tongues pierced, but that not everyone handles things the same way. A friend of mine got his tongue pierced and it was fine for a while. A week after the piercing, a large chunk of his skin turned green and popped out of the hole. This was totally disgusting. She knew the person also. I have told her that getting it done again would be the stupidest thing she could do.

I do not care how cool it may look to have a hole in the middle of your tongue. I think that it is disgusting, and it is not safe at all. People need all kinds of attention, so they go and do crazy things to their bodies. Well, my whole point was to try to make her understand that getting it done all over again is not only very hazardous to her health, but it is also very dumb. Your tongue muscle is very sensitive and any little prick that goes the wrong way can paralyze her muscle forever.

Needless to say, this story was the stimulus for considerable discussion. It was clear to the students that health was secondary to this writer's friend who wanted her tongue repierced. They believed the girl was foolish, especially when the student read about the large chunk of her friend's skin, which turned green and popped out of the hole. This story is an example of possible consequences that could forever maim this girl.

Value messages received through mentoring, namely, this young lady's story, are far more effective than pontification on the part of adults regarding the same topic.

Her story illustrates the mentor's point about encouraging thought awareness which results in understanding others without losing a sense of self. The reaction of her peers and the ensuing discussion validated her and contributed to her foundation of self- esteem and self-concept. Through her story she proved she is a good friend. She was able to provide wisdom to her friend, and her peers subsequently recognized her after she presented her story.

Tied up in the value systems of mentorees are their attitudes about life. While internal values, such as honesty, integrity, serenity, etc. are usually inviolate, attitudes and feelings about life can change. Attitudes are a choice, although usually an unconscious one.

One student's attitude of invulnerability, typical of a teenager, was challenged when he listened to his classmate's essay about hitchhiking.

He wrote, "The paper that had the biggest impact on me was the one that said not to pick up hitchhikers and how his uncle almost got killed by one." He could relate to this topic because he and his older brother have frequently hitchhiked during their summers here and during their visits to his homeland overseas. Hearing the story of a peer impacted this student's perception of his own safety.

This same type of story could be told by a mentor if he recognizes a potential problem for the mentoree.

Beliefs about one's ability to learn have a great effect on self-esteem. "The most debilitatingly effective way to produce passive failure is to have the learner attribute failure to ability, an attribution which is global, internal, uncontrollable, stable, and long term" (Jane Allen, *It's Never Too Late: Adolescents and Lifelong Literature)*, especially among potential high school dropouts.

An example of this sure way to produce passive failure is from an introspective, shy young man who was stuck in his own negative belief system. He believed he could not pass a test and proved it on a regular basis. However, through listening to the essays written by his peers, this student has "learned that some people were jealous of friends that were smarter but they [the people who were jealous] still found that they had an identity and [unfortunately] were not just book smart." It was an important concept for him to be able to connect with--the idea that a person can be book smart and still be his own person. Maybe "book smart" is something he can be, if he puts his mind to it. Now his tests are taken orally after school, and he has done considerably better. This young man is beginning to learn to change his self-concept about his learning abilities. Mentoring does impact self-concept in a very positive manner.

Self-knowledge is an additional benefit of mentoring and is an important part of self-esteem.

Another example of how a student learns about herself and her values through writing is a young lady who wrote her advice essay on listening. She began her paper by complaining that what really annoys her is "when people do not listen to me." By the end of the essay, she concluded that "maybe the problem is that I don't listen to people."

This is why mentors are encouraged to write in their Journals. Each entry is a step toward their own self-awareness. This is self-learning through writing, even before sharing. Similar self-learning happens through conversations with peer mentors.

Self-awareness is even more effective than instructor/mentor-directed awareness. There is another example of a student who learned in a self-correcting manner, who wrote a very strong paper and was able to correctly analyze it.

"My second paper was really a little out of line. I think I used the word *suck* too much. But the person I was inspired to write about means a whole lot to me. I don't think I read the paper the way I wanted to. When I started typing, I just typed what came to me and I thought it would be a real moving paper, but it came out all wrong."

Actually, his essay was a very effective paper, but not appropriate if an administrator were sitting in the room, therefore, inappropriate for this class. My reaction was neutral. This student took it upon himself to be critical of his overuse of the one word, an analysis that was more effective than if I had appeared offended.

PRESENTING AND LEARNING

Mentoring implies audience, even if it is an audience of one. An awareness of audience impacts how a mentoree speaks. One student not only felt better about herself after reading her papers aloud in class, but she also became aware of her listeners. "It made you feel like you not only worked for the teacher but that you worked for the entertainment of your classmates. So then you tend to do better, and show what you are really made of."

Shy students can experience increased self-esteem by the positive reactions of their mentor to their stories.

> Usually a student of few words, especially in his writing assignments, this student wrote an unusually long narrative about his reactions to reading his paper aloud. "I felt that writing, reading, and getting reactions from my advice was a good experience because it told me how to give advice; it improved my reading [aloud] skills and let people reply about the good points and bad points and what needs to be improved about the advice which I have written."

For him, reading aloud was painful, but he learned that "reading the advice improved how people talk to others and made them more fearless about reading in the future because of the applause each one got at the end."

He also learned the importance of effective reading. "Also reading something in a certain tone or voice can also get the reader's attention and make them more interested and involved in the advice or any essay." Most importantly, I believe he recognized that his opinions are respected by his peers. "Reactions from others was important because it got people involved and let them know that the reader respects his or her opinion."

The reactions of their peers affect every storyteller in some way. It was obvious that one student experienced pride in himself and in his writing because of his peers' reactions to his papers. He wrote:

> "But what really impressed me the most about my paper was myself. I actually saw myself differently while and after I read it. I learned a little something more about myself. I never had to actually write about something like giving advice, but now that I did, I feel even better.
>
> My peers' reactions helped. I liked that idea [of giving advice] because when someone gives advice, it means that they would probably follow it if they are in a similar

Gail A. Cassidy

situation, which helped me see the attitudes of some of my peers. It also, after writing, let me know that I was actually pretty good at giving advice."

More self-learning and self-understanding was evidenced by his statement.

"Reading it [his essay] out loud, though, made me realize how I really feel about some areas in terms of how I thought I felt. I guess sharing my stories helped me understand myself better as well as them."

This student's reaction is a perfect example of the positive affect peer mentoring has on student's self-esteem and self-concept.

Even the simplest recognition can have an effect on the student's self-concept.

One soft-spoken, timid student has rarely had a positive experience in a class, yet he wrote that it "felt good to write about giving advice because it's not every day I can explain how to become a good golfer. By writing this paper, I realized that I can give pretty good advice about something I know."

He was also "surprised at how the class reacted. It seemed like they liked hearing the advice and could all relate to it in some way. I also learned that my peers have many different ways of giving advice and they all seem very good at it."

The positive effects of validating reactions on students' self-esteem through presentation were also evident in one student's reaction. A master at speaking Eubonics, she stated,

"It made me feel as though people was really thinking about what I'm saying. Sharing my reaction was a great experience because the students listen. I [learned] I have a lot of talents that I didn't know about to [sic] they was written on the piece of paper."

One student, the class clown, realized a couple of things.

"One thing is that I do have the ability to make others laugh, even when I am not trying to be funny. I do not know if I like that or not, but I never knew that before. Also, I like the reactions I get whether they are good or bad. I just like the attention."

Feelings, positive or negative, frequently emanate from our values. If our values are demeaned, we experience anger, hostility, or some other negative reaction. Many students have experienced more than their share of negative reactions. If the feelings reinforce their values, they experience pleasure or some positive emotion.

The one student mentioned before felt validated by her peers after reading her essay on abortion. She wrote,

"The fact that there was a discussion on it after words [sic] was good too because it helped me see that I was not the only one who feels a certain way about this situation. It is kind of a problem for me to watch all of my friends throw their youth away, and talking about it helps me out a lot."

Mentoring is synonymous with empowerment of the individual who has shared a personal experience or expressed a personal opinion.

If *self-esteem*--a heightened belief in their abilities to achieve--and *confidence*--a feeling of equality--are the only two benefits from peer mentoring, then the process is more than worth the time and effort spent on it.

One female student, who barely passes any course, summarized beautifully,

"All in all, this was a fun reading assignment for me to do. And this is the first time in the longest time, maybe even the first ever, that I didn't mind reading out loud in front of my classmates. Because first of all it was something that I agreed on 100%. It was something that I wrote myself, and I had total confidence in it."

Learning about themselves through their writing or through their presenting and mirroring what their peers say are both positive ingredients in the recipe for heightened self-esteem. This same experience can now be had through a mentoring program.

ASSIGNMENT: In your Journal, write about the person or people you want to validate you, find your strengths. Who are they? How does it make you feel when you are validated?

S-A-V-E

This acronym, once mastered, could positively enhance all human interactions

The world has changed—technology, science, transportation, even foods have changed, but people have not changed. The four basic factors in this section are invaluable bits of knowledge about what all people respond to.

The one word that you will hear repeatedly is *S-A-V-E*, which is an acronym for **Safety, Acceptance, Validation** and **Enthusiasm.** The entire mentor training is based on these four letters, which are modifications of the principles in Maslow's Hierarchy of Needs.

As previously mentioned, Maslow believed that people have needs that follow one another in terms of importance. **Survival is first**. Man needs to survive which necessitates food, water, and shelter before he can think of anything else.

Second is Safety. Once man knows he can survive the wilderness, the outdoors, and have food to nourish his body, the next need is to be safe wherever he is. Once safe, the next need is **Acceptance**, something everyone desires. Acceptance leads to **Self-Esteem,** and Self--Esteem leads to **Self-Actualization**, which means making a difference in the world.

"S" is for SAFE

For this mentoring program, the **S** is for **Safe**, meaning every student's safety is assumed. When students go to school, they don't expect to be physically injured. Some schools are safer than others. In most schools, however, students can expect to be physically safe. Of course, exceptions exist related to physical safety -- Columbine, where so many students and teachers were killed; Virginia Tech, where a student went crazy and shot over 30 people. The tragedy at Sandy Hook and so many others. That is not the type of safety that is within your realm to control. As a mentor, you have very little, if any, influence over the general physical safety of the school.

What you do have some control over is your mentoree's **mental safety** when he or she is in your presence. In your presence there is no bullying. Everybody wants to feel safe, physically and mentally, and that means no "putting down," no ridiculing, no making fun of. All students have to feel safe from mental abuse.

Even teachers sometimes can be bullies. There was a young teacher where I taught who, if a student got the wrong answer in his math class, would have the offender tap his head 10 times while repeating the letters T--M backwards. Think about it, T--M backwards is M-T, M-T, M-T, M-T, M-T. What the student is saying is that his head is empty. I had young freshmen girls in the hallway stop me, crying. They had been in his class; and they knew if they got a wrong answer, they'd have to tap their heads and say M-T. That is bullying, and it is wrong.

ANOTHER EXAMPLE

One day I came into the classroom and immediately sensed something was wrong. There was one boy in that class who tended to be picked on incessantly, and, unfortunately, he usually did bring it on himself. He did weird things so the kids would pay attention to him.

Psychologists say that we all want to be recognized; we want attention. Even if it is bad attention, we want attention. We want people to know that we exist.

This young fellow gets wedgied in gym class and laughed at in the hall. This particular day I sensed something was wrong. I turned around and saw what was happening. I heard the quiet snickering and looked at the boy to see why.

He had cut his hair in the shape of a mushroom. Yes, a mushroom.

I could see why he was being tormented. His head looked like a mushroom, and it was funny looking; but I could not allow him to be ridiculed, even as I had to stifle my immediate reaction while calming down the classroom.

The point is he would do anything for attention, whether that attention is good or bad. If he had a mentor, perhaps his need for acceptance would be satisfied, and he would not continue to call unwelcomed attention to himself.

Later in the class, as I walked around the room, I glanced over his shoulder before he could block my view, and I saw in his notebook the words, "I want to kill them all" written at the top of the page. He was supposed to be writing a holiday story. This is a serious problem and one that I had to report to the guidance counselor. This bullied young man was a potential explosion.

Again, the first letter in **SAVE** is **S** for safety, mental safety, i.e., no laughing at, putting down or invalidating the person under any circumstance. Having you working with your mentoree is a form of validation right there. They know they're important because you are working with them.

ASSIGNMENT: In your Journal, write any instances where you saw someone being bullied or when you were bullied. How did you feel?

"A" is for ACCEPTANCE

The second letter in **SAVE** is **"A"** for **Acceptance.** Accept each mentoree as he/she is. Know that being different is a choice. No judgments allowed! Their actions could be a good choice or they could be a bad choice; either way, it's okay as long as what they do is not illegal or harmful to themselves or to others.

Their hair may not look like yours. Maybe it's a different color or a different shape, spiked, straight. A young girl on our block used to use magic marker to touch up her dyed black hair. She had light brown hair but she dyed it black. She had adopted the Gothic style, and her boyfriend had the Mohawk. His hair stood straight up and had a pink stripe, a green stripe, a yellow stripe. She looked different. She carried a lunch box, a child's lunch box, a little metal lunch box, sometimes a Mickey Mouse or a Donald Duck box. These were her handbags. All through high school she was different. However, when you talked with her, you felt she had wisdom beyond her years. She was a creative soul; she was different, and that's okay. She was one of the sharpest, kindest, most creative teens I had ever met.

Every human being wants to be accepted, but not necessarily by everyone, but at least by those whom they consider peers. For example, sports people may want to be accepted by others who play sports. Those interested in mechanics usually desire the acceptance of others with similar interests.

Part of your job as a mentor is to be accepting of your mentoree no matter what their interests, no matter how they dress, speak, and/or act.

Your mentoree may be different from you, and that's okay. You just accept them for who they are.

Now, the word again is **SAVE**. The **S is Safety**, the **A is Acceptance**, **V is**

Validation.

ASSIGNMENT: In your Journal, write about anyone you know who is "different?" How is that person regarded by his/her peers? How do you feel about this person?

"V" is for VALIDATION

Actress Marlee Matlin is the deaf actress who frequently appears on TV sitcoms and who sometimes speaks and sometimes uses sign language. She can say some words, but not clearly.

She tells the story about when she was 13 and told Henry Winkler, the Fonz from "Happy Days", that she wanted to act. He replied, "Do it and don't let anyone stand in your way."

She stated, "His validation just made it all the more true, and I haven't stopped thanking him since."

She is a successful actress even though she can't hear. She was on "Dancing with the Stars." She can't hear but she can feel the beat of the music.

The simple act of validation can make a huge difference in your mentoree's life. Find what they like and are good at doing, and let them know that you know.

Confucius said, "What the superior man seeks is in himself; what the small man seeks is in others."

What validation means is to check or provide the validity or accuracy of a person's characteristics, e.g., find what is special about your mentoree.

There's something special about everybody. Nobody is put on this Earth without having something special about them, and that's what you want to find.

Validation also means "to demonstrate the support or value of." In a healthy family, a child's feelings are validated.

"Validation" also means to make or declare legally valid, prove, substantiate, corroborate, verify, support, back up, bear out, lend force to, conform, justify, vindicate.

During my years teaching in high schools, I have seen kids divided into different segments: the nerds, the jocks, the mallers, etc. who totally change their opinion of one another just by listening to what is important to the others and finding that they can appreciate that person for just who he or she is.

These different perspectives emerged through a speaking class described at the end. Each student would get up and talk for two minutes. One of the comments at the end of the class was from a girl who said that what she learned during the class was not so much the speaking techniques, but more so was that there's something special about everyone. And that's what you'll do; you'll find what's special about your mentoree and tell him/her.

> **ASSIGNMENT: In your Journal, write about the person or people you want to validate you, find your strengths. Who are they? How does it make you feel when you are validated?**

"E" is for ENTHUSIASM

To repeat the **SAVE** acronym, again, **S** is **Safety, A** is **Acceptance, V** is **Validation,** and the **E** is **Enthusiasm.**

Emerson said, "Nothing great was ever achieved without enthusiasm." Pretend to be and you will be.

You may think, "What if I don't feel enthusiastic?" Dale Carnegie, author of *How to Win Friends and Influence People* said, "Act enthusiastic and you'll be enthusiastic."

Shakespeare said, "Assume a virtue if you have it not." Fake it till you make it. Just pretend and eventually you'll be the way you pretend. Assume that virtue you desire to have.

Enthusiasm guarantees your point will be positive. One of my favorite quotes is from Thomas Edison, "When a man dies, if he has passed enthusiasm along to his children, he has left them an estate of incalculable value."

In a business letter column, "The Pin Stripe Advisor," there was a letter to the Pin Stripe Advisor asking if a person is born with charisma or can charisma be developed? The advisor wrote in his column that **charisma is enthusiasm**. Whether it's loud or quiet, it's a characteristic that people gravitate to, and it can be developed on one's own. Enthusiastic people are fun to be around, and your mentoree will appreciate having an enthusiastic mentor.

"People rarely succeed unless they have fun in what they are doing." -- *Dale Carnegie*

We act as though comfort and luxury were the chief requirements of life, when all that we need to make us really **HAPPY** is something to be **ENTHUSIASTIC** about.

Enthusiasm breeds energy and if you are energetic, nothing is impossible. That is why it is said that nothing happens without enthusiasm.

Enthusiasm is so important that somebody has said, "If you don't feel enthusiastic, then fake your enthusiasm." That is because enthusiasm is infectious and your fake enthusiasm will make others enthusiastic (they don't know that your enthusiasm is fake) and their enthusiasm will, in turn, make you enthusiastic.

Mentors need to *show lively enthusiasm,* especially with an unmotivated mentoree. If the mentor shows no enthusiasm, the mentoree will reflect none. We "mirror" what we see, and this population is no exception to this rule. And if we don't feel it, again, as previously stated, take Shakespeare's advice, "Assume a virtue, if you have it not." Or, in the vernacular, "Fake it until you make it."

It is human nature to desire fun or pleasure over pain. Mentoring in an atmosphere of fun and/or pleasure enables young people to pay closer attention and retain direction better.

After a class where enthusiasm was discussed, a student came up and exclaimed with great enthusiasm, "But I can't be enthusiastic. I just can't!" But she just then was the perfect example of enthusiasm.

Why S-A-V-E Is Important

Mother Teresa's statement is so significant, "*There is that terrible hunger for love, to be wanted, to be loved, to be somebody to somebody.*"

Remember **S-A-V-E: Safety, Acceptance, Validation, Enthusiasm.** In these words are the secrets of success in whatever you do dealing with other people, all people, not just those you are mentoring.

The bottom line is we want to keep kids in school and out of gangs. We want to stop bullying in any form in or out of school, and we want to provide a safe mental place for kids to be in order to eliminate teen suicides.

Now you know the "why" of mentoring—why it is so vitally important to help those younger than you to gain confidence and self--respect. Once they have those qualities as a result of working with you, they'll be able to do well on their own.

PRACTICE ASSIGNMENT:

In order to mix up the groups, have everyone stand. The question is, "Guess the percentage of teens who need an alarm to wake up in the morning."

Line up according to your guess—low numbers on left; high numbers on the right. In other words, those who think 90% need an alarm, they would be at the far end of the group, starting with those who think only 2% need an alarm.

Once lined up from smallest percentage to highest, count off in three's. The first three is one group, the second three is another, and so on.

Within the group, the **first person answers the question, the second observes his/her body language, and the third judges voice.**

With each question, change responsibilities until all three have had an opportunity to observe a different aspect of the nonverbal communication.

Within the group, select one person to report to the group "safe atmosphere." The second person will report on the general impressions of body language, and a third person will report on voice.

Allow 5 minutes to discuss and 5 minutes to report on each of the following:

*   Why is it important to provide a "safe atmosphere" for mentorees?
*   Why is "acceptance" important?
*   Explain the significance of "validation."
*   Why is "enthusiasm" important?

Each group selects one person from the group to report on the responses to each of these questions.

*   How can we keep kids from dropping out?
*   How can you, the mentor, prepare them to be citizens of the world?
*   How can you get your mentorees to see the value within themselves?
*   What can you do to motivate them to learn?
*   How can you provide hope and opportunity?

Write the names of people in your life who have mentored you, believed in your, and/or encouraged you. You may have different people for different areas of your life.

DISCUSS.

> **ASSIGNMENT: Write what beliefs you have about yourself, your background, your abilities, your future, your physical, mental, and spiritual being. Share within your group.**

THE PHILOSOPHY OF KIDS MENTORING KIDS CONSISTS OF FIVE SPECIFIC PROVISIONS:

1. Provides a safe atmosphere--physically and mentally (no insults, no making someone wrong, no demeaning comments),
2. Validates students through their efforts by recognizing what they have done well or done correctly,
3. Establishes relevance--something they can relate to--in their assignments, and
4. Builds on their successes. This philosophy of learning also
5. Introduces the element of fun, a guaranteed way to encourage learning and growth.

Under the appropriate conditions, validating mentoring can be the foundation for

1. Improved self esteem
2. Self-concept
3. Improved interpersonal skills.

These benefits are not so surprising if one looks closely at the concepts inherent in the principles of human nature.

- *Mentoring* means taking a personal interest in a mentoree, supporting the paths he/she takes.
- Mentoring means helping the mentoree strive toward his highest aspirations, not only in career choice but also in the pursuit of happiness in his life.
- Mentors share their knowledge and experiences in the hope that their mentoree will reach a high level of achievement.
- Mentors promote the importance of responsibility both at home and away from it.
- Mentors care about the well-being of themselves and their families and model the behavior they want their mentorees to follow.
- Mentors receive the greatest gift--satisfaction in knowing they have made a difference.

Charles Engelhardt said it best: "The time to be happy is now. The place to be happy is here, and the way to be happy is by helping others."

ASSIGNMENT: Can you be enthusiastic whenever you desire to be? In your Journal, write how do you feel about Dale Carnegie's quote, "Act enthusiastic and you'll be enthusiastic?"

THE MENTOR'S CODE OF ETHICS

(The Baker's Dozen in Action)

Our values are determined by many factors in our lives: our parents, their style of upbringing, heritage, religious and ethnic backgrounds, socio-economic status, friends, teachers, television, and even political leaders we listen to on radio, social media and television. No two people are alike.

Most people agree on **three basic core values: HONESTY, INTEGRITY, AND MORALITY. These are essential for trust among friends.**

The following baker's dozen (13) were formulated as the result of decades of teaching students: high school, corporate employees of all levels, and school administrators in Lithuania.

Human Nature Law #1: SHOW RESPECT TO GET RESPECT

When I taught English to high school dropouts, ages 18 to 25, at our local Vocational-Technical school, I wrote about what I learned through the eyes of a teacher named Abby Foster. Here is what she learned from all of her combined teaching experiences.

At the beginning of the semester Abby heard from her fellow teachers about a young man who has been labeled a "real trouble-maker" in other classes. Abby's experience with Miguel was totally different.

On the first day of class, Abby walked into the room and the first thing she saw was a tall, lanky young man holding a very short girl's sneaker in his hand, her foot still attached. She was hobbling to maintain her upright position. Abby ran behind her to keep her from falling and realized, "This must be Miguel." It was.

The look in his eyes and the mischievousness of his expression told Abby that he was not a threat—maybe a pest but not a threat.

After weeks of observing the young man, Abby wrote her impressions of Miguel:

He has Michael Jordon's low key, teasing manner and warm, laughing eyes. I envy his laid-back personality. He could care less about making an impression. He's just Miguel, and he takes life and himself lightly--unless he is shown disrespect. Overall, he has a wonderful attitude.

Gail A. Cassidy

He loves to tease, especially the tiny little gal in his class who is one-half his size. He threatens to send the Smurfs to beat her up. She gets mad, and he keeps needling her—and she enjoys his attention.

One day in the middle of class, Miguel got up from his desk, walked to the front of the room and patted me on my head. Startled, I looked at him, and he whispered, "Miss, your hair was sticking up."

With hesitation, I stammered, "Thank you, Miguel."

Another time while everyone was quietly working in class, he yelled out with excited exuberance, "Miss, I know who you look like!"

"Who, Miguel? I asked."

"Santa's mom!"

"Thank you, Miguel," to which he sweetly uttered under his breath, "She's a cute little old lady."

This 6-foot 6 gentle giant is a delightful, spirited, handsome young man. He has a wonderful sense of humor. He's kind. He is a tease. He is a talker. He has personality galore. What he does not have is tolerance for anyone, including his teachers, who do not show him respect. When shown respect, he becomes a devotee.

Many of these high school dropouts have done things they should not have done; some have paid their dues through the penal system; some are awaiting their trials, and some still may not be clear between the boundaries of right and wrong, acceptable and unacceptable; appropriate and inappropriate.

Miguel is an example of an exuberant young man who at times is inappropriate, but he has good intentions. Abby believes that what made the difference in his behavior in her class was showing him respect as she expected respect from him--in spite of his sometimes- unusual behavior.

LESSON LEARNED: SHOW RESPECT TO GET RESPECT! People mirror other people. If they see hatred, they show hate. If they see respect, they show respect. "The Children's Creed" contains perfect examples.

CHILD'S CREED
CHILDREN LEARN WHAT THEY LIVE

If a child lives with criticism, he learns to condemn.
If a child lives with acceptance, he learns to love.
If a child lives with hostility, he learns to fight.
If a child lives with approval, he learns to like himself.
If a child lives with fear, he learns to be apprehensive.

If a child lives with recognition, he learns to have a goal.

If a child lives with pity, he learns to be sorry for himself.

If a child lives with fairness, he learns what justice is.

If a child lives with jealously, he learns to feel guilty.

If a child lives with honesty, he learns what truth is.

If a child lives with encouragement, he learns to be confident.

If a child lives with tolerance, he learns to be patient.

If a child lives with praise, he learns to be appreciative.

If a child lives with security, he learns to have faith in himself.

If a child lives with friendliness, he learns that a world is a nice place to live.

ASSIGNMENT: In your Journal, write what you have learned from reading about Miguel? Which line in the Child's Creed do you most relate to?

DISCUSS WITH CLASS.

Human Nature Law #2: BE NONJUDGMENTAL

On Abby's first cold January evening at the adult school for dropouts, she watched the young adults file into her classroom. The males were dressed in what looked like expensive jackets and either knitted caps pulled down over their ears or doo-rags or baseball caps on sideways. Although the room was toasty warm, they never took off their jackets for the entire class period. She later learned they feared their jackets would be stolen.

The females dressed provocatively--tight jeans, low-cut tops or tight sweaters, and, for the most part, they did not smile, at least not at her.

Abby's first impression was: *Here are some really rough, tough kids.* What she did not know were the stories each "at risk" student had. She had to be careful not to equate what she saw and/or heard with any impression of "bad." Here are a few other "first impressions."

- One of the first topics raised in class that evening was how fast they could get Abby's car to a "chop shop," a term Abby was unfamiliar with but quickly understood in context.
- As Abby was leaving the building her first night, in the parking lot all she could hear was the "f" bomb, "f----- this" and "f----- that," over and over. Finally, one of the students saw her and screamed at his friends, "Hey guys, watch your "f---ing language;" my "f---ing English teacher is here." He meant well, and it did strike her funny, though she did not show her reaction.

Gail A. Cassidy

- One of the first essays Abby read after the first night ended concluded with the following sentence: *"I shot him three times and got four years."* EEK!
- In one of Abby's classes was an 18-year-old girl, who has a five-year-old and a two-year-old with two different fathers, and she lives with her mom--and she is a real sweetheart!!

What Abby saw, read, and heard that first night made "being nonjudgmental" a very difficult concept to practice. As the semester progressed, however, she found all of the above words and behaviors to have no bearing at all on who they are or the probability of their potential success.

How they were treated or their perception of how they were treated, and how well they were doing had a far greater bearing on their success or lack thereof.

One young man did jail time for selling drugs. Was he a bad kid? Abby didn't think so after she heard his story

> He "tawks" tough - a "project" accent. He's a white kid with dreadlocks and baggy pants, and he has survived.
>
> When he was 12 years old, his single mother had a breakdown, and Omar became the breadwinner for the family. How could he best feed them all? Minimum wage at McDonalds (a job he was too young to get) or $500 a night on the corner selling drugs? He did what worked for him at the time, and he landed in jail. Poor choice, but how was he to know?

What's special about Omar? He's kind, gentle, caring, sweet - a truly good, loyal, nice person unwittingly put into a bad situation for which he has paid the piper.

> One day Abby was admonishing the class about keeping the room neat because the day teacher had complained again. In response to her exasperation, she heard a soft voice from the side of the room whisper, "Miss, ya wanus to take care of her?" asked Omar. Oh my!

He plays by the rules he learned as a child and as a child in jail.

What does Omar want to do with his life? He wants to counsel kids, so they don't end up as he did. Would he be good at it? You bet he would! He has sensitivity, sincerity, kindness, and meaningful experiences on which to draw. With the help of someone who believes in him, he may make it.

I hope he has an opportunity to travel that path. He deserves it, and he could really make a difference in the lives of potential lawbreaking teens. What a difference a a caring adult could make in Omar's life!

Some stories these young adults have experienced are almost unbelievable. Read about what Danny had to say about a can of soda.

The class was doing extemporaneous talks, which means Abby says a word, and they have to tell her a story about the word. She pointed to Danny and said, "soda." The soft spoken, reticent young man abruptly stood up and said vigorously, "I have a story" and proceeded with a tale that tore at everyone's heart.

"I went to the refrigerator to get a soda. My Dad came in and said, 'You better replace that. It's your mom's last soda.'

'I will,' I said, knowing she wasn't expected home for a couple of hours.

Before I even finished my soda, my mother came in, went to the refrigerator and yelled, 'Who took my soda?'"

Danny immediately assured her he would replace it right away.

"Now," he paused and said softly, "My dad loves to buy my mom rings with pretty stones. She wears rings on all of her fingers."

As Danny continued, he described how his mother with fingers on both hands bedecked with jeweled rings, pulled back her right fist and smashed him in the face, the rings tearing into his cheeks.

His head snapped to the right, and her left fist tore into the right side of his face with ferocity.

He slid down the wall to avoid further strikes, and she immediately started kicking him in the head with her spike-heeled shoes.

His father ran in and pulled her off of him.

Danny ran, which angered his father who ran after him and attempted to punch him. Danny jumped out of the way, and his father smashed his fist into the wall, jamming his wrist. He was ten times angrier now because he had bowling that night.

Danny quietly stated, "He still rolled 200."

The class questioned the veracity of his story, "Your mom wouldn't do that! Oh, come on!"

With eyes wide open and emotion still clutching his mind, Danny assured the class, "Oh yes she did! This happened!" and everyone believed him.

All for a can of soda! Danny related the story with emotion yet acceptance, as if "wow!" but "no big deal."

Gail A. Cassidy

An aside: Danny had missed a few classes earlier in the semester. Why? Abby learned that he had been treated in the hospital for attempted suicide. Would anyone wonder why? Again, what you see and hear may not be "what is."

LESSON LEARNED: BE NONJUDGMENTAL. Accept your mentorees as they are, and then provide the atmosphere for them to grow in a positive manner. Everybody has a story, and most will remain unknown to a teacher.

What you see and hear may not be what is. Clothes and words make an initial impression, but, having an impression and making a judgment are two different things. Judgment can cloud one's vision and frequently close doors.

"Accepting" a student or friend is a higher form of "being nonjudgmental." Making a judgment is responding to a stereotype in our own minds--doo-rags means "bad." Non-acceptance--being offended--is a personal response to a behavior or to words we believe to be offensive or wrong

Unfortunately, it is usually easier and perhaps safer to see faults in others rather than strengths. That is human nature. Finding a fault in someone else makes us feel better, for example, "He's fatter, louder, messier, etc.," if we can consider ourselves a wee bit superior by comparison.

ASSIGNMENT: Write and/or discuss times when you have formed a judgment only to find out you were wrong. Describe a time when you felt misjudged or misunderstood?

Human Nature Law #3: SEEK THE STRENGTHS IN EVERY STUDENT

- Help every student recognize his or her specialness.
- Remember that everyone desperately wants to feel special.
- See the invisible tattoo on every student's forehead that reads:
  "PLEASE MAKE ME FEEL IMPORTANT."

Show Abby a difficult teenager or young adult, and she will show you someone who doesn't feel appreciated and/or special. Get to know the person and you cannot help but see something that is distinctive about that person. It could be a sense of humor or warmth when dealing with a peer or sincerity or just a sparkle in their eyes.

Not everyone will fit the image of the perfect student, yet each possesses strengths, although he or she may not be aware of such distinctions.

Tall, angular, handsome George commands a room when he enters. He non-verbally demands the attention of the group. He dresses impeccably. Abby tells him he should put together a portfolio and go to a modeling agency. She can definitely picture him on the pages of a Lord & Taylor circular.

George is not unaware of his attractiveness. He hits on girls like Babe Ruth hit home runs.

> Underneath the good looks and confident attitude runs a river of anger, deep and well hidden. In response to a question in class, "What don't you like about your life right now?" Abby heard a barely audible but clearly angry response, "white people," which she didn't take personally, because she believes he doesn't put her in that large pool. She thinks she slides by in the category of teacher without color, and he knows she really cares for him.

> Another invisible aspect of George is his talent. He writes metaphorically. His words elicit pictures in the reader's mind. And he has the ability to tie them together without overkill. He is a naturally talented writer.

George is tough but vulnerable. He eyes, laughing one minute, unsure the next, give him away. He can be arrogant and act as if rules do not apply to him, yet Abby sees a caring, kind, young man under the facade of glamour and power he surrounds himself with. She sees a young man who, like most of us, needs respect and attention and needs to be a success in life. Beyond the bravado lies a sweetheart of a young man.

With George's ambition and natural abilities, his people skills, attitude, and confidence, Abby believes he will succeed in whatever field he chooses.

LESSONS LEARNED: SEEK THE STRENGTHS IN EVERY STUDENT. When Abby pointed out his strengths via a character sketch she had written about him, George was so surprised and delighted that someone had taken the time to write about him, he brought in his parents and aunts so they could meet her and see what she had written about him. (Three years after Abby had met his family at graduation, she read in the local paper the story of his stepmother's brutal slaying by his father.) A caring teacher, counselor, or mentor would be invaluable for George!

> One student who was encouraged only to look for the positives in others wrote: "The final and probably most important skill that I learned in this class was to only look for the positive in people. Because we were instructed to write down only positive things on our evaluation cards, picking out the good in people instead of bad has become second nature to me. This skill not only makes other people feel better, but it also reflects itself on my own disposition. When a person learns to see the positive in other people it brings a much more peaceful, optimistic outlook to the rest of the world around them." - Alessandra M.

Part of the problem in evaluating ourselves is we frequently do not see our own strengths; seeing strengths in others is easier than seeing them in ourselves. While a teacher may be aware of her student's needed areas of improvement, she may find that it is actually fun to seek the positives in them and in others she meets and let them know what she sees and why. The "why" validates the compliment.

> **ASSIGNMENT: In your Journal describe what strengths you see in yourself. This is for your eyes only. How would you like to improve?**

Human Nature Law #4: PROVIDE A SAFE ATMOSPHERE

Stephen Covey, in his book, *The Seven Habits of Highly Effective People*, talks about an eye doctor who was examining a patient who had complained that he couldn't see clearly. The eye doctor gave him his own glasses and said, "Try mine. They have worked for me for the last 25 years." The patient still could not see.

Abby encourages teachers to remember that each student brings with them his or her own prescriptive lenses through which they view the world. Everyone has different levels of vision--different prescriptions--according to their backgrounds and experiences in life. No one prescription fits all.

In order to provide a safe atmosphere for students, Abby believes a person must keep in mind that what they see and how they see may be different from what we may see and how we may see it.

Out of Abby's three classes one semester, one young man stands out--or rather *leaps* out in her mind. Timaro is that person--a real sweetheart! He is a delightful 24-year-old bundle of explosive energy that ignites at the slightest provocation--noise in the classroom, an "A" on a paper, an idea. He's like a "thought" jack-in-the-box or a drunken kangaroo--Abby never knew what would cause him to pop up next.

When he receives an "A" on a paper--and he receives many of them--he jumps up, goes to the other teachers in the room and enthusiastically demands, "See that! What does that say?" He is so proud, as well he should be.

He receives the "A's" because he has the ability to write from his heart. He also receives a second, usually lower grade for spelling and grammar, but that grade does not dampen his enthusiasm. He is conscientious and does all of his work. His enthusiasm is so refreshing and fun to watch!

The aspect of Timaro that Abby most admires is his sincerity. As he writes, so does he speak--from his heart, and he is easily wounded.

> One day Abby was announcing her "perfect students" which merely meant those who had all of their work in. Even though she had read Timaro's latest essay, he hadn't turned in the final copy; therefore, his name was not included in her announcement. She knew immediately that her omission had hurt him. "But, Miss, you saw my paper!" Abby wished she could take back her words.
>
> That incident revealed to her how hard Timaro works to be his best so he can get recognition for his efforts.

He confided in her that his father had always told him he wouldn't amount to anything--in variations that Timaro interpreted in the same way--he was a nothing and would always be a nothing.

Perhaps his father had been practicing tough love, hoping to motivate Timaro; but his method and assessment had an adverse effect on his son.

Timaro is unique. He is a tall, thin, handsome young man who wears his hair in dreadlocks adorned with five small, white puca shells tied into his hair. Each shell represents a special person in his life-- one being his child, another his "Boo," his special young lady, and another his mother.

Timaro is loud, outgoing, funny, and kind. He can be sitting quietly working and suddenly Abby will hear a startling loud "Miss!" even if she's standing right next to him. He has a question or impulse and acts on it immediately. This could be related to his energy level. He cannot be still for long. He could possibly be hyperactive. He apologizes if he feels he has been out of line--talking too much. He'll hush up others if he feels they have been out of line.

The class loves him. He can be outrageous, yet he is always kind. He'll tease Kareema and those around him, and they always respond with a laugh or a smile. He has his own seat but frequently changes in order to make another classmate feel special.

Timaro has definite leadership qualities, which just have to be pointed in the right direction. From what Abby hears him say, at least two major factors have molded him: (1) his father's constant invalidation/criticism and (2) the streets, which have taught him some harsh lessons. He has been, and is, in trouble with the law. Is locking him up the correct way to go for what he has done? The easy-going, outgoing exterior covers a deeply sensitive, genuinely nice person. Prison could drown that kind, inner person. Constructive direction would free the potential this young man possesses.

Timaro has the enthusiasm, the brains, and the sensitivity to be an outstanding teacher. Abby would love to see that happen. His creativity, his energy level, his leadership qualities, his sensitivity to others, his kindness, and his experiences in life all combine to potentially make him a positive influence on others.

Timaro will always have a special place in Abby's heart, and she hopes that all of his positive qualities will be given an opportunity to shine. He is one who could help make the world a better place in which to live.

There are two kinds of scars: external, which will heal; and internal, which leaves a scar. Ridicule from peers or teachers can leave scars. A safe atmosphere means a place where one can be himself without fear of ridicule.

A "safe atmosphere" does not preclude "boundaries." What a safe atmosphere does is allow a student to be himself. Providing this safety infers respect, non-judgment, boundaries, and acceptance.

Gail A. Cassidy

LESSON LEARNED: PROVIDE A SAFE ATMOSPHERE. By providing a safe place for students, they are unafraid to show their strengths and build upon them, especially with the guidance of a caring teacher.

A safe atmosphere can be set up by someone who truly believes in the concept of making everyone feel important, no matter what generation they represent. Because this concept of feeling important and accepted is the unconscious wish of everybody, it is difficult and uncomfortable to operate under any other canopy.

As mentioned previously, Abby was motivated to develop a course that incorporated acceptance and validation on a daily basis. She made her decision after reading the touching story of teacher in Minnesota who wrote about an unforgettable elementary student, Mark Eklund, a likable but frustrating student because of his inability to stay quiet in class. This story can be found under "Additional Courses" at the end of this book.

ASSIGNMENT: In your Journal, describe a time when you felt you were not in a safe environment. Was there anything you could do about it? If so, describe the situation.

Human Nature Law #5: KNOW THAT YOU CANNOT <u>NOT</u> COMMUNICATE, but what you think you see or hear may not be what is.

One young man in the back of Abby's class would never look at her or respond when she asked him a question. She believed he totally disliked her, but he never caused any trouble. He spoke to no one.

> One day Abby was handing out papers and was near his desk when she heard "Psst! Miss! Look at this, but don't say nothing." He handed her a paper, which she put into her briefcase and took home with her.
>
> His paper contained a poem about a girl he was deeply in love with. The poem was moving, tender, and beautifully written. Abby used post-it notes to point out what was particularly and specifically good about the poem and handed it back the next day. She was certain she had won him over.
>
> Wrong! Again, he avoided looking at her and never responded when she spoke to him.
>
> Weeks later, near the end of the semester, Abby heard another, "Psst! Miss! Look at this, but don't say nothing." He handed her a paper, which she read while standing next to his desk. This poem brought tears to her eyes, which he witnessed. The poem was about his attempt to end his life because his girl had left him.

When Abby went home, she again used post-it notes to comment on the excellence of his writing. She went on-line and found poetry writing contests, all of which she printed and gave him the next day.

When she returned his paper with the numerous post-it notes and the packet of contest forms, he took it, looked away, and never spoke to her again—ever.

This young man has the ability to express himself beautifully through poetry. The problem is Abby will never know if he uses his gift. Had he had the opportunity to work with someone who believed in him and encouraged him, he may have opened up. He may have been persuaded to utilize his writing ability.

Misinterpreting nonverbal communication is easy to do.

One young, vastly pregnant gal looked at Abby each day with disdain. She rolled her tee shirt up exposing her huge swollen belly and looked at Abby with the "Okay Miss, what are you going to do about it?" look on her face.

Abby never reacted.

After class one night she came to Abby's podium to ask a question about the final exam, when suddenly she bent over as she experienced a sharp contraction. Abby put her arm around her (forbidden action), and the gal instantly relaxed. Her baby was due in three weeks, and she wanted to know about the final exam, also scheduled in three weeks.

After that event, she came up every class period, and finally told Abby how scared she was because in three weeks, when the baby was born, she was going to be kicked out of the shelter.

Abby asked about her parents. She responded, "They won't take me in because I'm too black."

Her comment shocked Abby. Who knew the mental anguish this young gal was going through every single day! She trusted no one! Some adult - a caring adult, a preacher, a guidance counselor, someone, could have provided this young lady with guidance and validation.

LESSON LEARNED: YOU CANNOT <u>NOT</u> COMMUNICATE. The poet's body language told Abby he did not want her to pay attention to him. His actions told her an entirely different story.

The pregnant young lady also nonverbally told Abby to "stay away," and in reality, she responded to being comforted, a response she probably didn't expect to experience.

Gail A. Cassidy

Abby learned to go with her instincts. She learned that a non-response is also a response. She learned that what she viewed as a look of disdain was probably a fear of rejection posture.

As Stephen Covey says, "Try to understand before you are understood."

Misunderstanding someone else's demeanor, tone of voice, or words is so easy to do.

ASSIGNMENT: Write about a time when you were misunderstood or a time when you misunderstood someone else.

Human Nature Law #6: SET HIGH EXPECTATIONS

Another young man in the class was not only unaware of his gifts, but also he was convinced he was incompetent.

The first impression Abby had of Jack was that of a quiet, pensive young man. He is one who stays removed from the group until he analyzes the situation and feels secure enough to participate. He looks before he leaps.

What he doesn't know is that he is one of the most special students in the group. He is sincere. He is fun. He is personable. And he is bright, a lot brighter than he gives himself credit for.

> Jack regularly pulls the Marc Anthony at Caesar's funeral act. "I have come not to praise Caesar but to bury him," and then very cleverly lets the crowd understand Caesar's greatness. With Jack, it's "Miss, I can't do this. I can't write. I can't. I just can't do it!" He'll repeat this mantra numerous times, and then hands in a paper that is written quite nicely.
>
> For the next assignment, he starts all over again. "I can't do this, Miss. You have to understand; I just can't do it."

Jack is a genuinely nice person. He picks and chooses his friends carefully and, Abby would imagine, is loyal to a fault.

> He also has a wonderful sense of humor. One day Abby stepped into the hall for a few minutes, returned, and there was Jack standing there with a devilish grin on his face. "Missing anything, Miss?" he asked. Abby looked at him blankly as he began to unload his pockets--her stopwatch, bell, clicker, pencil, pen, marker--and she hadn't even noticed. He chuckled as he left the room.

Jack is good with people. He's kind, gentle, sensitive, easy-going. He's good looking. He's fun and funny. Abby could easily see him owning his own deli or someplace where he'd deal with people on a regular basis. That's his strength--his understanding of people and his ability to relate to them and make them feel good. Whatever he chooses, Abby hopes he remembers that he is one very special young man, and he can do whatever he wants to do.

LESSON LEARNED: SET HIGH EXPECTATIONS. The story is true about the new teacher who thought the locker list from 140-160 was the list of IQs in her class and she treated them accordingly, and they performed accordingly. What she didn't know was that she had the lowest performing group at that grade level. Because she treated them as if they were bright, set high expectations, they acted as if they were bright.

> **ASSIGNMENT: Can you give a specific example when you misjudged someone's ability or a time when you helped someone realize what was special about themselves?**

Human Nature Law #7: MAKE SINCERITY YOUR #1 PRIORITY

An essential component of every relationship is sincerity. The sincerity of the teacher is paramount. Students can pick out a phony in very short order, especially street-smart kids who have "been around." Trying to be "one of the guys" does not work, and it affects the students' perception of the teacher's sincerity.

> Abby had a very handsome young man in her class who happened to be a delightful con man. A few weeks passed before she realized how frequently she had been duped. For example, one speaking assignment required him to sell a product. He chose cologne. On his evaluation card, Abby wrote, "I don't have a clue what he's saying." I knew it wasn't cologne he was selling. I could tell by the response of the class that it had to be something illegal. When Abby challenged him, he smiled broadly and said, "Okay, I'll sell ice cream."

Same scenario--couldn't understand a thing he said. He was pitching drugs and having a ball doing it, especially when he knew that I didn't know the terminology.

What's so special about this?

This young man's mental adroitness is incredible. He relishes the spotlight, doesn't allow criticism (Abby's) to dampen his spirits and generally maintains a positive attitude. His stature and extraordinary good looks facilitate his success at the con game, a phrase Abby uses with affection.

Those are the positives. While Abby doesn't want to encourage him to be a "flim flam" man, she does want to encourage him to use his talents in a positive way. But how? His ability to speak "around her" would be useful in negotiating or selling

Success will probably elude this young man as long as he lacks sincerity. He is bright. He does have charm. He does have warmth. He doesn't have sincerity; therefore, he cannot be trusted and won't be trusted once people get past the facade one time.

Abby learned that a teacher can quickly learn the lingo used for drugs and lifestyle, but she believes that "Playing dumb" can work to a teacher's advantage. Anyone can learn a lot by being "out of it" or "not cool." Anyone can play dumb and still be sincere.

Trying to sound and talk like the students does not work to a teacher's advantage. It is okay to be "older" and "not cool." Attempts to be one of them is each teacher's own desire to be accepted. They just have to get over that!

LESSON LEARNED: MAKE SINCERITY YOUR #1 PRIORITY. As important as it is to encourage a student to be him- or herself, it is equally important for the teacher to be himself or herself. Someone in their 20's working with teens is a decade older and already has some "dated" singing idols and music favorites. Whether a teacher is in their 30's, 40's, 50's or higher, it's okay to be who they are regardless of the generation to which they belong.

Each generation is unique, and those from other age groups who try to "fit in" by using "hip" jargon may sound foolish. Be sincere to your students as well as to yourself.

Sincerity with others and sincerity to oneself is even more effective when cushioned with warmth. In her book, *Your Child's Self-Esteem*, Dorothy Corkhill Briggs says that the most important factor for a person's self-esteem is the degree of warmth experienced by the child, rather than any particular techniques of child training. Warmth is an integral part of making a person feel important; it is an integral part of feeling accepted.

Anyone can master human relation skills, but they are merely tools of manipulation if **lacking sincerity.**

ASSIGNMENT: What experience have you had with people who are not sincere? Have you ever been insincere? Explain.

Human Nature Law #8: BE SENSITIVE

Sensitivity is one characteristic of the students that Abby had noticed numerous times when dealing with the "at risk" population. She realized that once they trust you, they become very sensitive to how you act and react, especially when they feel your "sensitivity" toward them.

As part of a *Discover Your Passion* assignment, Abby had the students list words that they believed described themselves. Almost everyone wrote the word "nice." Some chose words such as "loyal," "shy," "outgoing," "talented," plus many more.

Primarily, they wanted Abby to know they were nice people in spite of what has happened to them, what they had done, and where they are currently.

Abby then asked them to write three words they would like to have describe them. For example, she said, "I would like to have people describe me as "skinny." She had said that same line for 16 years teaching her *Discover Your Passion* course to adults, and people always chuckled and went on with their assignment.

This time the class stopped and looked at her. One boy said, "Why you wanna be skinny, Miss? You got a husband."

Another boy said, "You look fine, Miss."

Now Abby was embarrassed. She was only trying to be funny.

Then the last young man said, "Miss, ain't you heard that thick chicks is better than skinny ones?"

Abby loved it. It's all perspective! She realized she doesn't have a weight problem; she's just a thick chick. Because they had accepted her, they were sensitive to her being hurt in any way.

Abby believes that showing the same sensitivity about their challenges in life will do more for their self-esteem than anything anyone could do.

One invaluable lesson Abby learned about the importance of being sensitive came as a result of her less-than-neutral response to a student from Columbia who said it was most important that he have a hot meal on the table when he gets home from work at 9:30 every night, and he does not want it microwaved.

The girls in the class verbally attacked him. They told him he was inconsiderate of his mother, that he was a male chauvinist, and that he was insensitive.

Abby erred in agreeing with them, a transgression she suspected but later understood when she realized how different his culture is from hers.

Through her experiences, Abby learned that teachers can further validate students by being sensitive to their backgrounds and cultures, by recognizing the importance of their individual perspectives, by validating feelings and encouraging connections, and by accepting each student as important in his or her own right.

One evening, while the class was working quietly, Keon asked aloud, "Miss, if I gave you $500,000, would you quit teaching?"

Abby responded immediately with a resounding "Yes."

He looked disappointed. He was silent. She thought that he had hoped she wasn't able to be "bought out." Abby believed she had let him down.

Gail A. Cassidy

A few minutes later she teasingly asked, "Keon, if I gave you $500,000, would you go straight?" He smiled his sweetest smile and said, "Ah, I'd like to have something 'legit,' Miss, but I'll always have something on the side. Keeps life exciting."

Where does a teacher go from here? She can't give him the desire to stay out of trouble. His father has been in jail since he was a young boy, so that potential role model doesn't exist for him.

In Keon, Abby sees kindness and sensitivity. She sees a genuinely nice person: respectful, bright, a leader, charismatic, fun. On the negative side, she would say he is not reliable or dependable and perhaps not always trustworthy. Yet, overall, he has so much potential. In jail he has no potential, and in that setting all of his assets turn to liabilities.

Keon is aware of his strengths. He is a lady's man--very flirtatious and perhaps lacking sincerity in those moments. Whatever path he chooses, he just has to keep in mind that he has choices, all of which have consequences--good or bad.

LESSON LEARNED: BE SENSITIVE. As mentioned under "Show Respect to Get Respect," having someone pat my head in the middle of class seemed inappropriate. However, under the circumstance with this student, it was appropriate; it was just unexpected.

Being put on the spot by an unexpected question taught Abby a lesson, i.e., "I must think before I speak."

Teachers have to be sensitive to the fact that the person they are working with does not have the same background and experiences that they have had in life, therefore, they cannot expect them to react in a similar manner.

Abby learned that showing respect, being nonjudgmental and accepting, providing a safe atmosphere and seeking their strengths are very important actions, but showing sensitivity is the ultimate compliment to an individual.

> **ASSIGNMENT: Write about when someone was less than sensitive to you. Are you aware of being insensitive to others? If so, describe.**

Human Nature Law #9: SET BOUNDARIES

The home and street experiences of most high school dropouts are responsible for many of the survival characteristics this population has adopted to "get by" in life. Some students have a difficult time learning that there are times when they do have to follow the rules; and if they choose not to, then they receive the consequences. A perfect example of this is the following young lady's story.

Julia is cute, lively, and certainly outgoing--traits which would appear, and which Abby originally believed, would make her an asset to the class. She volunteers to read aloud. She answers questions when asked. She brings enthusiasm to the class. These are the delightful aspects of Julia.

She is also a chatterbox with her best friend, as many her age are. The first day of class, after asking the girls numerous times to stop talking, Abby just separated them--problem solved, or so she thought.

The problem with Julia in class is not her talking; it's her belief that she does not have to follow any rules but her own. She will talk to her friend across people while the teacher is teaching, if she so desires.

During a test, where she was allowed to work with the person next to her, she turned around and gave answers to the boys at the table behind her, because she wanted to. Abby asked her not to work with anyone but her assigned partner.

She continued the same exact behavior in spite of being asked three times not to talk because this is a test. She finally complied, turned around to her desk, and then called out the answer to the test question so all of the class could hear. Is that acceptable behavior in an adult school? She was asked to leave.

On her way out, Julia uttered, "If you think my attitude will be better on Monday, you are in for a big surprise." Is that a threat?

When Abby returned the following week, Julia showed up for class. Abby took her into the hall to talk to her. She asked her to explain why she had acted as she did during the test, and Julia explained that the boys behind her asked her for the answer. Abby asked her why she called out the answer, and she said, "Oh, did everyone hear me?" She knew they had, especially when, for fairness, Abby repeated it for the few who were not paying attention.

Abby told her she felt that she was an asset to the class, that she has more personality than three people and that Abby genuinely enjoyed her as a student; but she could not put up with that behavior. She told Julia she would have to follow the rules if she wants to be in this class.

Julia appeared contrite and agreed to follow the rules, so Abby relented and allowed her back into the classroom. Abby reminded her that she was on thin ice and the next infraction would cost her her seat in class, for which there is a waiting list. She seemed to understand.

Three days later, and Abby's first time in front of the class again, although only to take roll and observe her student teacher, Julia again is sitting with her friend, talking. Abby reminded them they could not ever sit together. They pushed their chairs apart so another person could have moved in the space, although no one did.

Miss Jackson, the student teacher in training, taught the class, while Abby worked in the back of the class, then the side of the room. As Miss Jackson was teaching, Abby was distracted from her work by chattering. Guess who?

Julia and her friend had pushed their chairs back together again and were talking like magpies, totally ignoring the teacher. As they continued talking, Abby couldn't say anything because of the teaching going on in front of the room. When Miss Jackson paused, Abby jumped in and asked Julia to see her.

With anger, Julia approached Abby. Abby reminded her that she had asked at the beginning of class that she and her friend were not to sit together, and Abby reminded her of their agreement for her being back in class.

Rather than apologize or take responsibility for her action, Julia proceeded to tell Abby that she was out of line for speaking to her regarding her actions in this class because she was not the teacher of this class. She was not in charge; and if Miss Jackson didn't like what she was doing, it was up to Miss Jackson to tell her, because it was her class, not Abby's.

At this point, Abby found listening to her defiance and arrogance to be a bit much, so she calmly interjected, "And you are no longer a part of this class and may leave." She left, announcing to the class in anger that she had been kicked out.

This young lady has so many wonderful attributes going for her, all of which will count for little if she continues with her belief that she does not have to follow the rules or be sensitive to other people. She obviously cannot tolerate not having her own way. To her, the only rules she has to follow are those of her own making or liking. She believes she is "entitled" to act however she pleases.

Part of the growing/maturing process, as Abby sees it, is learning how to interact with others, how to "play the game." Abby would have failed to do her job had she allowed Julia to maintain and act out on that belief in Abby's class. Someone has to say "no" to this young lady. If every student believes and acts as she does, there would be pandemonium in the classroom.

Abby sees her as a spoiled child who has tantrums if she does not get her way. Abby hopes she recognizes that limits are there for a reason, and sometimes she just has to adjust. She hasn't learned that yet.

Abby believes that if a student is not cooperative, have the principal switch this child to another classroom. If the second teacher has the same experience, the student should be dismissed. Boundaries do have to be set.

LESSON LEARNED: SET BOUNDARIES. If everyone in society did what they wanted to do, when they wanted to do it, the world would be in chaos. Small children find life easier when boundaries are set, in spite of their protests. Students have to recognize and follow the rules and regulations of society in order to succeed.

Abby also learned that being "right" does not always work, as illustrated in the following ditty:

"Here lies the body of William Jay,
Who died maintaining his right of way.
He was right, dead right, as he sped along,
But he is just as dead as if he were wrong."

ASSIGNMENT: Of what importance is "setting boundaries" to you? Be specific!

Human Nature Law #10: HAVE FUN/FEEL GOOD

Abby believes that almost anything can be made fun. She recalls the stories she has read regarding the famous Pike Place Fish Market in Seattle, Washington, where the employees throw the fish to one another, sing, laugh, and have a ball--selling fish! What a delightful place to work!

According to Abby, teaching should be a pleasurable experience. She wants kids to enjoy the lesson, find the humor, and have a good time. Human nature seeks pleasure and avoids pain. Sometimes school can feel "painful."

Specifically, one of the least favorite lessons Abby had to teach to high school students each week was vocabulary. That is, it was unpopular until she divided the students into groups, assigned each group 5 words and had them come up with a skit with only 15 minutes preparation time.

Vocabulary day came to be one of the most enjoyable days of the week. The skits were creative and fun—sometimes belly-laugh fun, and the test scores went up on average by 10 points in every class.

"Having fun" means "feeling good." Abby's question is always, "How can we make our lives better than they are now?" Or better yet, "How can we make our students' lives better than they are now?"

Abby hopes that some of the tips in the following paragraph will help everyone live a happier life, especially in dealing with other people.

To begin with, Abby believes there are three things each of us needs for ourselves. We need food—wholesome and nutritious—to nourish our bodies. We need shelter—a safe place to live. We need validation—someone to let us know we are important to the world. When we have these three essentials—food, shelter, and validation—in our lives, we can work on being the best that we can be

Gail A. Cassidy

Abby suggested that
TO HAVE FUN, LIVE THE BEST LIFE YOU CAN
BY BEING THE BEST THAT YOU CAN BE

To feel GOOD, choose and experience
any of these "feel-good" emotions:
Passion
Bliss
Happiness
Reverence
Joy
Trust
Optimism
Inspiration
Harmony
Appreciation

Abby recommends that most importantly, every day, we express
GRATITUDE and seek BEAUTY, validate people, look for their positives,
and show everyone kindness, appreciation, and respect.

Thoughts are choices and can be positive or negative. It is
up to the individual to make the selection!

A recent *Washington Post* article chronicles the importance of laughter in the lives of Carl Reiner, Mel Brooks, Betty White, Norman Lear, and Dick Van Dyke, all comedians in their 90's. Carl Reiner, 97, believes humor has enriched his life and boosted his longevity.

One commonality everyone shares is the enjoyment of laughter. It makes you feel good. It relieves tension. Studies suggest that laughter can improve health and possibly stave off disease, thereby extending life. It also eases stress and helps the ill cope with their sickness and pain.

"A friendly sense of humor will bless you with better social relations as well as coping skills, and the reduced risk of dying early," says Sven Svebak, professor emeritus at the Norwegian University of Science and Technology, who has studied the health impact of humor for more than 50 years. "A friendly sense of humor acts like shock absorbers in a car a mental shock absorber in everyday life to help us cope better with a range of frustrations, hassles, and irritations."

Laughter and humor are great prescriptions for these high school dropouts who suffer from their own range of frustrations, hassles and irritations.

Another recommendation for humor comes from Edward Creagan, professor of medical oncology at the Mayo Clinic College of Medicine and Science. He says, "When people are funny, they attract other people, and community connectedness is the social currency for longevity."

A great motto for everyone to adopt is "Live, Laugh, Love, and Learn!"

On the other hand,
To feel BAD, choose
Judgment and/or negativity through feelings of
Revenge
Excuses
Procrastination
Anger
Justification
Gossip
Hate
Ill Will
Blame
Sickness
Gloom
Despair
Criticism
Hatred
Restrictions
Anxiety
Fear
Shame

These feelings equal depression, sadness, "I don't feel good."

Abby believes that if everyone's ultimate goal is to feel good, what better way than to have fun while working to become a better person and helping someone else also become a better person!

LESSON LEARNED: HAVE FUN/FEEL GOOD! Enjoy!

ASSIGNMENT: Who do you most like being around? Why? Look at the people in your life—who makes you feel good? How? Who makes you feel bad? How? How would people write about you in response to this question?

Human Nature Law #11: SMILE: It warms a room.

Abby's recommendations:

People gravitate toward a smile. It is welcoming. It is validating.

Make it a point to smile and laugh every single day. It feels good and is good for you mentally and physically.

"A smile is happiness you'll find right under your nose." - Tom Wilson

Become aware of how, when you smile, you automatically feel better. When you are smiling, it is hard to feel sad or angry.

There is a physiological reason why smiling makes you feel better. Put your shoulders back, your head held high, and smile. You will feel good because the blood flows more readily to your brain when your shoulders are back and your head held high, so smiling comes naturally and feels good.

> **ASSIGNMENT: How often do you smile? Do you do it naturally or only on special occasions? Be aware of how you FEEL when you smile, especially in contrast to a frown.**

Human Nature Law #12: BE (OR ACT) ENTHUSIASTIC about everything you do.

More of Abby's recommendations:

Enthusiasm is contagious; it carries over to your students.

Because we have already covered enthusiasm, I'll include just one quote from Maxwell Maltz:

> "You must create [enthusiasm] yourself without waiting for someone to thrust it upon you. Enthusiasm is a thought turned into a performance; it is the kinetic energy that propels you to your destination. Enthusiasm implies that you believe in yourself, that you concentrate with courage, that you practice self-discipline, that you have a dream, that you see victory in the distance."

> **ASSIGNMENT: Since we have covered this previously, I'll remind you of Dale Carnegie's words: • Act enthusiastic and you'll be enthusiastic.**

Human Nature Law #13: Remember, PEOPLE HAVE TWO BASIC NEEDS: TO KNOW THEY ARE LOVABLE AND TO KNOW THEY ARE WORTHWHILE.

> **ASSIGNMENT: Write about your reaction(s) to Human Nature Law #13.**

COMMUNICATION SKILLS

YOU CANNOT <u>NOT</u> COMMUNICATE

Let's review what we have already covered.

- Why is it important that we have a mentoring program here?
- We want kids to do their best in school, but how?
- We want to prepare them for good citizenship, but how?
- We want to teach them to value themselves.
- We want to motivate them.
- We want to provide a safe haven to grow and to learn.
- We want to give them life--enhancing skills, but how?

How do you develop character, provide hope, provide opportunity, provide security?

Many of the answers can be found in the acronym **S-A-V-E** that we recently covered.

S is for Safety, the mental safety that prevents any bullying during their time with you. Bullying means teasing, making fun of, putting down in any way, shape or form. So, the S is the safe environment with you.

The **A is the Acceptance** of them exactly as they are.

The **V is the Validation,** finding out what's special about them. Anybody who works on their natural talents and abilities will do well because they believe in themselves.

And, of course, **E is for Enthusiasm.**

Gail A. Cassidy

COMMUNICATION PROBLEMS

What impact would mentoring have on the school if all students were mentored, if all students felt safe? Do you think the mentorees' grades would improve? Would how a class acts and reacts change?

Productive students would impact their schools. And, in the long range, the graduates are the ones who will impact the country.

This session will cover two broad topics: **Nonverbal Communication and Human Relations Skills.**

Nonverbal communication problems arise because we cannot **NOT** communicate. Think about it. You cannot **NOT** communicate—it is that simple.

By not responding, you're communicating. By staring ahead, you're communicating. The grimace, the frown, the happiness – it's all communication. You cannot NOT communicate.

When you go home and someone in your family is angry, can you tell without them uttering a word? You can tell just by observing them.

If the first communication problem is we cannot NOT communicate, the second communication problem is we don't all see things in the same way. We can look at the same object and see something different according to our experiences. If everyone were assigned to look out the window and stare at the tree in the courtyard, would everyone see the same thing?

ASSIGNMENT: Class Assignment: Look out the window and, for ten minutes, write what you see. Share your responses. You will notice that some will discuss the bark of the tree or perhaps the limbs or leaves or type of tree. Some may discuss the grass or flowers beneath the tree. Having two people agree on exactly what they observe would be unusual. The point is you cannot NOT communicate.

BODY LANGUAGE

Fifty-five percent of the message that you get when you encounter somebody is by what you see. Again, **fifty-five percent comes from observing the physical body.**

To repeat the example previously used, when you go home and someone that you live with is very angry with you, can you tell without them uttering one word? The answer is no doubt, "Yes." One glance reveals their body language which reveals their emotions. You may see their stiffness, the way they look at you, their facial expression, but you know by looking at someone if they're annoyed or if they're happy.

Although fifty-five percent of the message comes from body language, what you see may not be what is.

> For example, there is the story of two men walking across a field when they feel the ground shake. They turn around and see a bull bearing down on them. One friend runs to the closest tree, throws his legs around the branch and pulls himself up. His friend runs down the hill with the bull getting closer and closer.
>
> All of a sudden, the man disappears. There was a cave at the bottom of the hill.
>
> His friend in the tree watches closely and suddenly sees his friend come out of the cave. The bull attacks, and he runs back in. A few minutes later, he comes out again, the bull attacks, and he runs back in.
>
> This continues for quite some time—man out, bull attacks, man in.
>
> His friend can't understand why he doesn't just stay in the cave.
>
> Finally, the bull gets tired, walks away and disappears over the hill. The friend climbs out of tree and meets up with his friend near the cave and asks, "Why didn't you stay in the cave?"
>
> His friend said, "I couldn't! **There was a bear in the cave.**"
>
> **The point is: What you think you see may not be what is.**

Suppose a friend fails to say hello or sounds brusque when you see her, does that mean she is angry with you? Not necessarily! Remember, he or she could have come from a place where there was a bear in the cave.

To further illustrate the problem with communication is a fun and true story about Clyde Von Olson and his talking horse.

At the turn of the century, there was a man, Herr Von Olston, who trained his horse, Hans, to do simple arithmetic by tapping his front hoof. Such was the animal's prodigious ability that its fame spread quickly throughout Europe. His ability was reported on and suggested that it was an intriguing and baffling act. Not only could clever Hans perform addition, subtraction, multiplication and division, he was even able to solve problems containing fractions and factors.

Without Von Olson uttering a word, Hans could count out the size of the audience or tap the number wearing hats or glasses or respond to any other counting question asked. Hans quickly attracted the attention of scientists, and a commission was set up to establish whether this was a case of clever trickery or equine genius.

Hans performed before professors of psychology and physiology, a circus owner, vets, calvary officers. Von Oston was banished from the room, but Hans was still able to provide the right answers with apparent ease. The commission announced itself satisfied that the horse really could understand arithmetic.

But a second, rather more perceptive board of inquiry put an end to that belief. They asked the horse questions to which no single member of the audience knew the answer. For instance, Von Oston was asked to whisper a number into the animal's right ear while another member of the audience whispered a second number into his left ear. Under these conditions, Hans remained dumb. The explanation was simple.

Hans was not especially bright, but he was especially observant and highly skilled at reading human body language.

When Hans started to answer a question, the audience became tense. That tenseness was only a slight increase, too slight for the human eye to detect, but perfectly noticeable to the horse.

Then, when the correct number of hoof beats had been tapped out, they would relax again. Hans noticed the change in nonverbal behavior and stopped tapping.

His cleverness was not in his ability to verbalize or understand verbal commands, but in his ability to respond to almost imperceptible and unconscious movements on the part of those surrounding him.

As human beings, we too react as Hans reacted. We detect the change in someone's body language, even though we may not be aware of it.

Did you ever notice that when you are talking, you tend to nod your head to make a point? In the future, be aware of your listeners. You will notice that they, too, nod their heads when you're speaking. It is their way of validating what you say.

As mentors working with a mentoree, you might notice as you are talking, that he or she is nodding. If you become aware that they are not nodding, you may have to communicate in a different manner in order to get them onboard with you.

Also, when you're talking, youu will notice the listener's eyes will go from your one eye to the other eye to your nose—eye, eye, nose. During an interview for a job or for college, the interviewer's eyes generally go from eye to eye to nose. This is done unconsciously; no one thinks about it. These findings are results from hidden cameras focused on interviewers and the person being interviewed.

If you start feeling uncomfortable as you're being interviewed, notice the interviewer's eyes. If he or she deviates from the eye--eye--nose pattern and does eye-eye-chin or mouth, that's almost a flirtation; and it's something that may make you feel uncomfortable, even if you are not aware of the pattern.

Be aware of how someone is looking at you; notice where their eyes are directed. Being aware is helpful when working with a mentoree who initially may be uncomfortable with you.

Another subtle body language action is the eyebrow flash. When you see a friend you like, your eyebrows automatically go up. When you are flirting, your eyebrows flash up and stay up longer than usual. Notice what happens when you see somebody who catches your eye. Your eyebrows do stay up a little bit longer. It's an unconscious reaction. It's not something that you think about. It's just something you do.

An example of the subconscious nature of the eyebrow flash was described in an incident at a police station where two suspects being interrogated in separate rooms swore they did not know each other. Hours later, they were being moved to another cell, passed each other in the hall, and their eyebrows flashed up momentarily, enough so to alert the officers that these two men did indeed know one another.

When you become more aware of body language and what it means, you can adapt in order to make a better impact on your mentoree.

Even something as the space between two people is significant. When you stand talking to somebody, you are usually about 18 inches apart, especially if you are in the United States. If you move closer, it's uncomfortable for both parties.

In some countries, the custom is to move closer. In the Mideast, you will see men talking to each other eye to eye with their toes just about touching. In the United States, having somebody stand in your space is uncomfortable.

If you have a mentoree from another country, a Columbian student, for example, they, by custom, stand more closely than the 18 inches Americans like when they are talking. In this instance, you just have to adjust to make yourself feel comfortable.

Gail A. Cassidy

Body language communication extends to the shaking of hands where frequently a first impression is made. A firm handshake indicates confidence. A limp, dead fish handshake tells the other person that you're not as confident, that you aren't as strong. In between a firm shake and a limp handshake could be a pump--handle shake or a delicate fingertip shake or a bruiser, bone--crusher shake.

What you want to aim for is a confident shake which gives the impression that you are confident. When you shake your mentoree's hand, shake with confidence and look him in the eye. If your mentoree does not shake with confidence in return, ask him/her to because you are the one who is guiding them; you're the one who's making a difference in their lives.

> **ASSIGNMENT: This would be a good time to have the class stand and have them go up and down the rows, shaking hands with their fellow students. Afterwards, write what you learned about the significance of the handshake. Identify the type of handshakes you experienced: firm (confident), limp (dead-fish), active (pump-handle), delicate (fingertips), bruiser (bone crusher).**

BODY LANGUAGE CUES

WHAT <u>COULD</u> THE FOLLOWING GESTURES MEAN?

1. Tapping of fingers
2. Shrugging of shoulders
3. Wringing of hands
4. Clenched fist(s)
5. Open hands, palms up,
6. Arms crossed on chest
7. Walking fast, chin held high, arms swinging
8. Shuffling walk, head low
9. Palm held to cheek
10. Stroking chin
11. Touching, rubbing nose
12. Hands on Hips
13. Head titled to side
14. Steepling of hands
15. Peering over glasses
16. Pacing
17. Pinching bridge of nose in
18. Sitting on edge of chair
19. Crossed leg, kicking motion
20. Pointing of index finger
21. Poor eye contact
22. Sideways glance
23. Unbuttoned coat
24. Rubbing eyes
25. Playing with hair
26. Hand covering mouth

Notice how many different meanings each could have.
Body language cues are one part of the message.

There are no wrong answers!

NEXT TO EACH NUMBER, WRITE THE FIRST LETTER OF WHAT EACH ACTION REPRESENTS TO YOU, USING THE FOLLOWING AS A GUIDE:

(D) -- Defensiveness

(S) -- Suspicion

(C) -- Confidence
(Frustration)

(R) -- Reflective

(O) -- Openness and Cooperation

(I) -- Insecurity and Nervousness

Notice how many different meanings each could have. Body
language cues are one part of the message.

ASSIGNMENT: Assign students to act out various gestures: CONFIDENT, INSECURE, ELATED, DEPRESSED, SAD, SCARED, HAPPY, HURT, WORRIED, GUILTY, BORED, PLAYFUL, CALM, HOPEFUL. How many can be guessed correctly.

WRITE your reactions to this exercise. List as many places as possible where you can SHOW a more positive attitude. What could this mean to you?

Gail A. Cassidy

VOICE
Remember, you cannot NOT communicate!

Thirty-eight percent of the message is conveyed through the voice, through the tone, through the loudness of the voice.

> Mark Twain who was known for his salty language was a master of the use of his voice, even when swearing. One day, he was getting dressed for an important affair he had to attend. He reached into his armoire for a shirt, and as he put it on, the button popped off, and he swore. He took out the next one and found a broken button. He threw it on the bed and swore again. He took out the last shirt and found it was totally missing a button. He slammed the shirt onto the bed and swore like a sailor. He used every foul word he knew.

> What stopped his tirade was seeing his sweet wife standing in the doorway with her hands on her hips and looking very upset.

> In order to teach him a lesson, she walked into the middle of the room and repeated every single foul word he had spoken.

> When she finished, she turned and saw him leaning against the doorjamb with a twinkle in his eye. He calmly said, You've got the words right, but you don't have the music."

The point is your voice reveals your emotion. When you hear somebody swear, it's usually with anger in the voice. If you were to swear without the anger behind it, it's not the same thing.

If you were to use the word spaghetti, you could make it sound foul by saying, "What the spaghetti do you want?" You know what word was intended just from the tone of the voice, from the pitch of the voice, from the way it was said.

The thirty-eight percent of what you hear includes the tone. It could be that your voice is high. It could be the pace—very fast or very slow. The tone, the pitch, the fastness, slowness of speech are all part of the message.

For example, if I say, "Nice tie!" is that a compliment? The words are okay, "It's a nice tie," the tone could indicate that I'm making fun of it, and you know that already by my voice.

Again, if I say, "Nice tie," I may not be complimenting the tie; I could be making fun of the tie. The message is found in the tone of voice.

If your mother ever says to you, "I don't like your tone of voice," and you can say, "All I said was…" and you repeat what you said, the words might be fine; it's the tone of voice that conveys the message you trying to convey.

If I were to say, "Get out of here," how many different meanings—humor, anger, annoyance--could I convey? Give it a try.

Think about the simple phrase, "Good morning." How many different ways can you say those two words? Try it. There are dozens of ways to say "good morning." Proof of this statement is having each student say "Good Morning" each with a different emotion conveyed.

Why does that make a difference? When you greet somebody in the morning with the oft-used phrase, "Hello," their response may not be what you expected. They may respond to the voice that you used—happy, sad, disgusted, angry, or any other emotion.

How many definitions or interpretations of the following sentence could there be? "**I didn't say she stole his wallet.**"

There are seven words and possibly seven definitions according to which word in the sentence is stressed. By stressing the first word,

- **I** didn't say…" means it was someone else who said it.
- By stressing the second word, I **didn't**… indicates denial.
- Emphasize the third word, I didn't **say**… indicates denial.
- By emphasizing **he** could mean you meant "she."
- I didn't say she **stole**…could imply she just borrowed.
- I didn't say she **his** could mean it was really hers.
- I didn't say she stole his **wallet**; it was really I just borrowed a few dollars.

The emphasis on each word gives the sentence a different meaning, according to which one it is. You know that, and you use it automatically. This is brought to your awareness only because you want to be aware of how your mentoree is feeling when you are speaking to them.

ASSIGNMENT: How many different meanings can be found in the following sentences?

- **I am happy to see you.**
- **Your sister is smart.**
- **I wouldn't want your job.**
- **I think you are great.**

Write your reaction to what you learned about voice and tell how your awareness will affect you in the future.

WORDS

Seven percent of a message comes from the words. For example, "Describe a duck that's ready to eat."

What do you visualize when hearing those words?

Some may say they see a swan, a beautiful white swan that is ready to eat the food on the pond.

Some of you might say golden brown. If your bird is roasted for dinner, ready to eat, you chose brown, and then you'd be right.

If you chose white, and you're thinking of a duck on a pond, you're right.

Both are correct. The point is, the language must be clear.

Another silly example is of a woman exchanging a bird for her husband. A husband bought his wife a parakeet from a pet store. She wanted a canary.

The next day she went into the pet store and said, "I'd like to exchange this parakeet for my husband."

The pet store owner immediately responded, "We don't trade husbands for birds." Chuckle, chuckle.

Be aware of language; be aware of what interpretation your words could have.

ASSIGNMENT: In your Journal, list statement(s) you have spoken or heard that were unclear? What have you learned from this exercise?

TRY TO UNDERSTAND BEFORE
YOU ARE UNDERSTOOD

In order to be clearly understood, we all must be aware of our communication skills and of how misinterpretations could take place, especially when working with a mentoree who might be feeling uncomfortable to begin with.

> To make this point is a brief story from Steven Covey's *Seven Habits for Highly Effective People.* A man went to his eye doctor and told him the world was blurry. The optometrist took off his glasses and said, "Here, use mine. They have worked for me for twenty--five years."
>
> Guess what? The man still could not see.

The point is one answer is not for all. We all have our own prescriptions. We have to remember that each person brings his or her own prescriptive lenses through which they view the world. We all have different levels of vision, different prescriptions according to our backgrounds and experiences in life. No one prescription fits all.

And that is why I so appreciate the serenity prayer: *"God, grant me the serenity to accept the things I cannot change, courage to change the things I can, and the wisdom to know the difference."*

The things that you cannot change include the color of your eyes unless you buy colored contacts, but you cannot change them. You cannot change your height, your ethnicity, your family, your natural abilities.

But there are some things you can change. If you do not like your attitude, you can change it. If you do not like the grades, you can change them. If you do not like your body image, you can change that.

Just know what you can and what you cannot change. Make sure you know the difference.

> Another example of the importance of the *Serenity Prayer* is found in a story from Steven Covey's *Seven Habits of Highly Effective People.*

There is a training squadron on sea maneuvers in heavy weather for several days in the cold, choppy waters of the North Sea. One naval seaman was serving on the lead battleship and was on watch on the bridge as night fell.

> Shortly after dark, the lookout on the wing of a bridge reported a light bearing downward on starboard bow. The visibility was poor with patchy fog, so the captain remained on the bridge, keeping an eye on all directions.

Shortly after dark, the lookout said, "Light bearing on the starboard bow."

"Is it moving or steady?" the captain called out.

The lookout responded, "Steady, Captain," which meant they were on a dangerous collision course with that ship.

The captain then called to the signalman, "Signal that ship, 'We are on a collision course. Advise, you change course 20 degrees.'"

Back came a signal, "Advisable for you to change course 20 degrees."

The captain said, "Send, 'I'm a captain! Change course 20 degrees.'"

"I'm a seamen second class," came the reply, "You had better change course 20 degrees."

By this time, the captain was furious. He spat out, "Send, I'm a battleship; change course 20 degrees."

Back came the flashing light, "I'm a lighthouse!" and we changed course.

The point is *take the time to understand rather than be understood.*

Know what you can change and what you can't. If you are making a point with your mentoree, listen carefully to see what they are really saying. They may be on the same page with you, and they might not be.

Just remember, "Grant me the serenity to accept the things I cannot change, courage to change the things I can, and the wisdom to know the difference."

ASSIGNMENT: What was your reaction to the optometrist story and the sea captain story?

HUMAN RELATION SKILLS

Of greatest importance is **making sure that sincerity is your number one priority. Always be sincere.**

HUMAN RELATIONS STACK

"Stacking" is a great mnemonic device to use to remember items, names, dates, or points in a talk. Once you know the points you want to make, you then develop each point into a picture. For example, if you wanted to remember 9 human relations principles, you could picture the following:

(The items underlined are those you want to have the participants clearly see.)

In your mind's eye, picture an <u>ice statue</u> of a <u>cheerleader</u> with <u>headphones</u> on. Look closely and you'll see, as in a cartoon, <u>bubbles</u> coming out of her head, indicating she is thinking. What she is thinking about is a <u>thermostat</u>, so she won't melt. In her <u>praying hands</u> is a huge <u>candy bar</u>. On the wrapper of the candy bar is a big <u>C</u> and a <u>plus sign</u> (<u>+</u>).

The pictures are explained as follows:

<u>Ice Statue:</u> Accept people as they are.

<u>Cheerleader:</u> Be enthusiastic in all you do.

<u>Headphones:</u> Listen. It is the greatest compliment you can pay someone.

<u>Bubbles:</u> Thoughts. Change your thoughts and you change your world. -Emerson.

<u>Thermostat:</u> You can't control what happens to you, but you can always control your reactions.

<u>Praying hands:</u> Accept what is, e.g., Serenity Prayer.

<u>Candy bar:</u> Treat others as you wish to be treated.

<u>C:</u> Do not criticize other people. No one ever appreciates it.

<u>+ sign:</u> Look for the positives in everyone.

REMEMBER: If you always do what you've always done, you'll always get what you've always got.

Most importantly, all of this is done with sincerity. You can use these principles to manipulate people, but **then they are not human relation principles**; they're merely tools of manipulation. If you use them with sincerity, they are human relation principles.

Gail A. Cassidy

The basic needs everybody has, no matter what age, is to know they are lovable and to know they are worthwhile. When you are working with a mentoree, if you can enable them to feel those two things—to know they are lovable and worthwhile— they will blossom. They will do well!

ASSIGNMENT: In your Journal (1) write about the stacking process and its value to you in other courses, and (2) what is your reaction to the nine Human Relation principles? How and with whom do you intend to use them?

REVIEW OF SECTION TWO

Think about and discuss these questions:

- How can we keep kids from dropping out of school?
- How can you, the mentor, prepare them to be citizens of the world?
- How can you get them to see the value within themselves?
- What can you do to motivate them to learn?
- How can you provide hope and opportunity?

This entire Section has been about mastering people skills which can be used with your mentors, your teachers, your friends and with anyone in your life.

If you think about it, all you have to do is implement the word **S-A-V-E** and don't tolerate bullying. Why do people bully? They bully because they want to make themselves feel good, which means they have an inadequacy of their own. If someone bullies somebody else, that's their own inadequacy—to show they are bigger or stronger. All of those questions can be addressed by **S-A-V-E:** Provide a **safe** atmosphere, **accept** them as they are, **validate** them, which means find what is special about them, and do it with **enthusiasm**.

The **Code of Ethics** are applicable to anyone you interact with in life.

Communication skills, including awareness of body language, voice, and words are major success tools for anyone who applies them.

The nine **Human Relation Skills** can improve your relationships with everyone.

ASSIGNMENT: In your Journal, list the people in your life who have mentored you, believed in you, encouraged you. How did they do it?

WHO ELSE IN YOUR LIFE ENCOURAGES YOU? HOW?

WHAT BELIEFS DO YOU HAVE ABOUT YOURSELF, YOUR BACKGROUND, YOUR ABILITIES, YOUR FUTURE?

The final question is "WHY DO YOU WANT TO BECOME A MENTOR?

Share your responses in the next session.

Gail A. Cassidy

PART THREE

ESSENTIAL SKILLS:

Questioning
Listening
Tolerations
Belief

OVERVIEW OF PART THREE

The essence of mentoring is mastering the art of listening, the least taught communication skill.

In this section, mentors will learn how to establish rapport with their mentoree.

Listening skills are important in all areas of life. These skills can be used at home, in school, and with friends.

Being aware of Tolerations, things people put up with, is important in understanding each mentoree.

Knowing how others view the world, their belief system, is important in understanding not only the mentoree but also people interacted with every day.

EFFECTIVE QUESTIONING TECHNIQUES

ESTABLISHING RAPPORT

When you meet and begin talking to your mentor, the first step is to establish rapport.

Sit as your mentoree is sitting. If he is sitting back in the chair, you sit back in the chair. You are imitating his body language. He will remain unaware of what you are doing but will feel comfortable with you.

You want to gain trust, and this is one way to do it. Practice at home with a parent or sibling. If they prop their elbow on the table, you do the same. If they smile, you smile. If they cross their arms, do the same. Unless you are trying to be obvious, they will be unaware of what you are doing. They will feel as if you as like them, and we all like people who are like us.

If you are being interviewed for college or for a job, do the same thing. If the interviewer feels comfortable with you, he or she may relate to you more. You can even emulate the loudness, tone, and pitch of the voice. A person with a soft voice could be offended by a strident voice. Watch his pace. Fast talkers like fast talkers; slow talkers like slow talkers. Your goal is to establish rapport, and that is exactly what you are doing!

QUESTIONING

- **ASK**
- **PARAPHRASE**
- **PAUSE**
- **QUESTION**

When initiating a question, make sure it is an open-ended question. In other words, if I ask, "Did you go to the game last night?" I will get a "yes" or "no" response. That is a closed-ended question.

If I start a question with "Who" or "What" or "Where" or "Why" or "When" or "How," I will get more than a one-word response. Those are open-ended questions and are guaranteed to start the conversation. If you ask, "How did you like the game last night?" you will be an entirely different answer, assuming they attended the game.

Whatever answer you receive, you could paraphrase (reword or summarize) what they said without exactly duplicating what you heard. For example, if you asked, "Why did you drop out of Striker's class," your mentoree might respond, "I just couldn't understand what he was covering." A paraphrase could sound like, "You felt the information was difficult to understand" or "He wasn't clear in explaining the material." However you respond, the mentoree will clarify your interpretation of what he meant.

"**Pause**" is difficult at the beginning. If you see a movie star being interviewed on television, you will notice that the reporter often pauses after the star gives an answer.

The point is silence is loud, so loud that the star may fill it in, thus providing additional information the reporter never would have gotten. Silence is a powerful tool.

"**Question**" refers to continuing your search for information by asking a follow-up question. Repeat this process until you are comfortable doing it and get the information you are seeking.

One of the best to become proficient with your questioning skills is to practice.

PRACTICE

Divide into groups of three. Take three minutes to discuss each of the following questions. Come to a consensus that you can share with the class. Appoint a spokesperson for each question so everyone has a turn to respond.

As each speaker reports to the class, keep a list of what you liked about how they responded insofar as body language and voice are concerned. Absolutely no negative responses allowed.

Share what you liked with each person who spoke. Remember, you are judging them strictly on body language and voice.

- **How can you motive your mentorees to do better in school?**
- **How can you help mentorees see their own value?**
- **How can you provide a safe haven for your mentoree?**

ASSIGNMENT: Report findings to group

THE MENTOR'S COMMUNICATION SECRET

LISTENING

A major component of validating mentoring is *listening*, a communication skill that is rarely taught. Listening means hearing the words while reading between the lines.

Listening is a primary key to effective mentoring. In fact, active listening suggests that you, the listener, have a strongly composed sense of self--you project self-confidence.

If listening is to be beneficial, there must be some mutual acceptance, in other words, non-judgment of one another's point of view. Listening is necessary in order to experience the feeling of equality. It validates a person's perceptions. By actually listening to mentorees, we legitimize their voices.

To communicate effectively, we have to learn the perspectives of others. What better way than through listening empathetically!

When respectful listening prevails in a mentoring situation, open conversations about improving one's self can begin. All are created equal and all can be heard. Under these conditions, more mentorees will want to participate.

Mentorees say what they feel. Thus, what they have to say is not the result of a script that is carefully rehearsed in advance. Rather their words grow out of what they have experienced in the world, good or bad.

As a mentor, listening is one of the most important skills to master.

TO BE AN EFFECTIVE LISTENER:

1. **BE SILENT**

Say nothing while the mentoree is responding; don't try to fill the gap of silence with your words--a favorite tactic used by reporters as they interview celebrities. Avoid thinking about your response while your mentoree is speaking. Pause before you respond.

2. **HEAR THE WORDS THAT ARE SPOKEN AND THOSE THAT ARE NOT**

Hear not only the words spoken, but also hear the tone, inflection, rate of speed, energy, and emotion. The words may be positive; for example, "Nice tie." The inflection may indicate ridicule of the tie.

3. LISTEN WITH YOUR SENSES

When you "feel" that the words you are hearing contain more than the message, question the mentoree to see if she is willing to reveal more than she said. Strengthen your "inner" hearing skills.

4. REFLECT BACK WHAT YOU HEAR

Say to the mentoree, "In other words, you feel you were treated poorly," even if the words did not say that directly. The mentoree will either confirm or deny your interpretation. "Reflecting back" what you hear is a great way to clarify communication.

5. FURTHER CLARIFICATION

Get more information in three areas: What happened? How are you feeling? What do you want? Don't move on until you are satisfied with the response.

6. PROMPTS

THINGS TO LISTEN FOR

1. AUTHENTICITY AND TRUTH: LISTEN FOR TONE AND LANGUAGE

Does the mentoree really mean what he is saying? What is really talking through him? Himself? The Past? Needs? Fear? Love? Parents? Friends?

2. TRUE DESIRES

Listen for progress and level of commitment to the program and to their goals. Do they know what they really want?

3. FEARS

Listen for concerns, less than desirable behaviors and blocks.
Through questioning, find the source of their fears and have them develop a plan to alleviate these concerns.

4. SUPPORT

Are they missing personal or financial support? Are there areas where more support could be given, and who would provide that for them?

5. POSITIVES

When possible, concentrate and elaborate on the positives in their lives.
Have them point out how their lives are better than they were before.

Gail A. Cassidy

Point out progress and/or growth from previous session.

6. **YOUR REACTIONS TO YOUR MENTOREE**

How are you reacting to your mentoree? How is your reaction affecting your mentoring? Point out to your mentoree specific ways in which you are developing as a result of this relationship.

LISTENING GUIDELINES:

- **Be silent**
- **Hear words spoken and not spoken**
- **Listen with your senses**
- **Reflect back what you hear**
- **Ask for further clarification**
- **Use prompts**

This is a good time to talk about listening skills. You may think, "Well, everybody can listen." The majority of people can; however, listening is the most neglected and least taught form of communication, and we can improve our listening skills. We will cover specific ways to listen.

Today we are going to talk about Listening. We all do it, but remember, listening is more than hearing.

But, first of all, learn **how to be an effective listener.** Listening is something we all do, but many of us do not all do it effectively. Listening is the one form of communication that is not covered as a form of communication. How to speak well is taught, but how to listen well is not.

The first step in effective listening is silence. Immediately after you have asked a question or are in a discussion, just be silent. Say nothing while the mentoree is thinking of a response or is actually responding. Do not try to fill the gap of silence with your words. As mentioned before, silence is a tactic used by reporters when they interview celebrities. Nothing is louder than silence which motivates the celebrity to respond. To repeat, silence is deafening; it's too loud. Avoid thinking about what you're going to say while your mentoree is speaking. Pause before you respond.

The second recommendation is to hear the words spoken and those unspoken. Hear not only the words spoken, but also hear the tone, the inflection, the rate of speed, the energy, the emotion that comes with the words. The words may be positive, i.e., "Nice tie," but, as mentioned previously, the inflection might indicate ridicule of the tie. The message does not come just from the words, as you already know; it comes 38 percent from the voice-the inflection, the tone-and 55 percent from the body language that accompanies the words. So, hear the words spoken and those not spoken.

Three, listen with your senses. When you feel that the words you are hearing contain more than the message, question the mentoree to see if he or she is willing to reveal more than what was said. Strengthen your inner hearing skills.

The more you talk to your mentoree, the more proficient you will become doing this. Initially, you might not be comfortable as you become aware, because listening is something you have done all of your life; and you have never been aware that you are listening. You might even say to somebody, "Well, I know you hear me, but have you listened to me? You might hear my words, but have you listened to me?"

And one way to show that you are listening is **Four, reflect back what you hear.** In other words, you feel you were treated poorly, even if the words did not say that directly. The mentoree will either confirm or deny your interpretation. Reflecting back (called paraphrasing) what you hear is a great way to clarify communication.

Five, ask for further clarification. Get more information in three areas: What happened? How are you feeling? What do you want? Don't move on until you're satisfied with the response. Again, the three areas are: What happened? How are you feeling? What do you want?

Six, get the mentoree to say more. "Really?" "Are you sure?" "Tell me more." "That's very interesting." Keep going. Keep the mentoree on track. "I'd like to hear more about …" One way to hear more is not to interject too much, even though you might want to.

What you want to listen for as the mentoree is speaking is authenticity and truth. Listen for tone and language. Does the mentoree really mean what he or she is saying? What is really talking through them? Themselves? The past? Their needs? Their fears? Love? Parents? Friends?

THINGS TO LISTEN FOR:

- **Authenticity and Truth (tone and language)**
- **True desires**
- **Fears**
- **Support**
- **Positives**
- **Your reactions to mentoree**

We may not purposefully mislead somebody, but we may want to maintain the façade of somebody who's not bothered by whatever is going on in our life; however, the tone and the body language (Authenticity) will reveal more than the words.

Listen for their **true desires.** Listen for progress and their level of commitment to the program and to their goals. Do they know what they really want? If you were to ask, "Do you know what you want in life?" Most people do not know. If you are an accomplished singer, you know you want to be a singer, but most of us don't know what we want in life. If, in response to your questions, your mentoree is telling you one thing, listen carefully. Watch his body; listen to his tone of voice.

Another thing to listen for is **fear.** Listen for concerns, less than desirable behaviors and blocks. Through questioning, find the source of their fears and have them develop a plan to alleviate these concerns.

Gail A. Cassidy

We all have fears, and it is said in some circles that the one thing that blocks us from getting what we want in life is fear. Fear of being embarrassed, fear of failing, fear of not being capable are examples of common fears.

Another thing to listen for is **support.** Are they missing personal or financial support? Are there areas where more support could be given? And who would provide that for them? If you don't know and if you feel that there is an area in which they are missing support, ask your guidance counselor.

Another thing to listen to are the **positives.** When possible, contribute and elaborate on the positives in their lives. Have them point out how their lives are better than they were before they began the mentoring program. Focus on the good things that are happening in their lives. If they start focusing more on that, perhaps more good will be manifested. Point out progress and/or growth from the previous session.

Also, listen for your reactions to the mentoree. How are you reacting? How is your reaction affecting your mentoring? Do you like your mentoree? On occasion, a mismatch can be made which is neither the fault of the mentor or mentoree. If you feel this way after a few sessions, see your guidance counselor. You don't want to stay in a relationship that is not working.

Where possible, point out to your mentoree specific ways in which you are developing as a result of this relationship. What a compliment to the mentoree if he feels that you are benefiting as a result of working with him.

Again, you listen for authenticity and truth via tone and language; you listen to their true desires, their fears, the support they may have or not have, the positives in their lives, and your own reactions.

Remember the words: "Change your thoughts and you change your world." (William James, psychologist) That seems so simple, but so true. How and what you think is under your control. Thoughts pop into your mind, but if you are focusing on something negative, something bad that happened, guess what – more bad is likely to come along. If, on the other hand, you focus on the positive, you attract more positive.

Everyone knows people who see the world in a positive light and people who always see the negative. Which one do you prefer being around? How do you see your life? And how does your view of life reflect in your mentoree?

Responsibility is as responsibility does. **Everybody needs validation through acceptance and encouragement; and that is what you as a mentor are doing. You are validating through acceptance and encouragement.**

ASSIGNMENT: At home practice what you have learned in this section with family members. What worked and what didn't?

TOLERATIONS

There is something called "Tolerations." **Tolerations are what you put up with.** What stress or restrictions do you have in your environment? Are there things that you are tolerating that you don't want to? What is your mentoree tolerating, and how is that affecting his or her behavior?

Step one is to identify areas you put up with; for example, situations, behaviors ---- yours or others, your environment, your body, your feelings, your problems, pressures, family members, clutter, traffic, computer, neighbors, pets, restrictions, stress, inadequacies, events, friends, your job, your situation in life.

What are you putting up with? As long as you have tolerations, you won't have complete peace of mind, and you will have stress. If your goal is to be the best that you can be in every way, start being aware of and listing every toleration in your life.

You have to be aware. Step one to positive change is always awareness. You can help your mentoree become aware also.

Once you're aware of a toleration, then you have an opportunity to make a plan. Once the thing, person or situation is brought to the forefront of your mind, you will be better prepared to deal with it.

For example, if someone's always picking on you and you tolerate it, you are under stress. You have two choices: leave the vicinity of the person or disconnect—mentally check—out when that person is on your back.

I can give the example of my mother, and I loved her dearly. I talked to her every Sunday night after I left home, and she would always tell me what I should be doing. I would be annoyed because she was still treating me like a child. Finally, I learned to disconnect. I could hear her words, but I did not react emotionally. That takes time, and it takes a lot of effort; but if you are being upset and unrightly and unjustly so, just disconnect. The person probably believes their nit-picking is for your own good, and you know they care; but they're still a source of stress.

You cannot always control what happens to you, but you can always control how you react. Do not allow anybody to push your buttons. This is a lesson that you can master and pass on to your mentoree. Again, you cannot control what happens to you, but you can always control how you react.

When speaking to a group, I usually choose three dissimilar-looking people in an audience. One could be tough looking, one could appear very sweet, someone could be very shy. I say to them, "Suppose I kick each one in the shins, this person, this person, this person. Will you all react in the same way?" They laugh. One might get up and kick me back; one might cry and run out of the room; and one might just be horribly disappointed. We don't always have the same reaction, but we have a choice.

Gail A. Cassidy

You can control how you react. When you master controlling your reactions, you can help your mentoree control his or her reactions also.

PRACTICE IN SMALL GROUPS AND DISCUSS THE FOLLOWING:

Within the group, the **first** person answers the question, the **second** observes his/her body language, and the **third** judges voice.

With each question, change responsibilities until all three have had an opportunity to observe a different aspect of the nonverbal communication.

Within the group, select one person to report to the group "safe atmosphere." The second person will report on the general impressions of body language, and a third person will report on voice.

Allow 5 minutes to discuss and 5 minutes to report on each of the following:

- **What would you like a mentor to ask you if you were the one being mentored?**
- **What is the most valuable tool you have learned?**
- **Why should you paraphrase, pause, and ask a question when talking to your mentoree?**

ASSIGNMENT: What did you learn about "Tolerations" that you were unaware of before? What are your tolerations?

THE IMPORTANCE OF BELIEF

The importance of belief is stated differently in the following famous quotation, "What the mind can see and believe, it can achieve." Napoleon Hill wrote his book, *Think and Grow Rich,* in 1937, and the concept is still as true today as it was then.

For example, if your mind can come up with an idea that you believe in, chances are you will be able to achieve it. You might want to be a singer, but if you can't carry a tune, you're not going to *believe* you can be a singer. Maybe you are not good in math. If that is so, you probably are not going to be a scientist or an engineer; however, you will undoubtedly be great doing something else.

If your mind believes you can do something, you can achieve it. Henry Ford who is known for developing the automated assembly line for cars, said, "If you think you can or you think you can't, you're right." Again, "If you think you can or if you think you can't, you're right." That is the power of belief.

Belief impacts not only human beings, but also the animal kingdom, even insects. For example, if you catch flees and put them in a jar, they will jump up and hit their heads, jump up and hit their heads on the lid until finally they realize they can't get out. After a few futile attempts to escape, they sit on the bottom of the jar. You can take the lid off of the jar; you can move the jar around; the flees will not jump again. Why?

Because they believe they can't get out.

From a much larger point of view is the belief of an elephant. At the circus you may see a little elephant tied to a stake in the ground by a little, thin chain that goes around his leg. As the elephant grows, getting bigger and bigger and bigger, finally maturing into a huge pachyderm, weighing up to 15,000 pounds, he is still tied to a stake in the ground with a little, thin chain. He could pull the stake right out of the ground, but he doesn't. Why? Because he believes he can't. He won't do what he can't believe he can do. This is the power of belief.

We all have a conscious mind which we are using right now to think, to make decisions, to daydream. We also have a subconscious mind where habits and beliefs reside. You don't have to think about how to brush your teeth—it's a habit—no thought required, and it is a belief that you can do it without any thought. The subconscious mind does what it is trained to do; it does not know the different between real and the imaginary.

At some point in your lives, you will be interviewed, whether for college or for a job. Before you go on an interview, take a moment and mentally rehearse the scene just like actors and athletes do and tell yourself, "I'm great for this place." Do it over and over again just before the interview. See the interviewer responding favorably to you. Don't take my word for it, give it a try. You have nothing to lose and everything to gain. The point is: believe you will do well, and in all probability, you will do well.

Scholars and philosophers throughout history have stated that whatever you believe with conviction you can achieve. Don't be like the poor elephant and go through your life stuck because of a limiting belief that you were given or developed years ago. Take charge of your life and live it to the fullest. You deserve the best.

Another example of the power of belief comes from the work of Dr. Herbert Benson, a brain researcher from Harvard University. He was involved with a meditation movement in the 1970's when Transcendental Meditation became popular. Students paid $300 to take the course and get a nonsense word like gunnum – gunnum or loogoo, a word with two syllables that were repeated over and over again to put the student into a meditative state. Dr. Benson found out that a person could say "one, two, one, two," and achieve the same exact effect.

He has devoted his career to the study of the mind. On one of his trips to Tibet, Dr. Benson observed how spiritual men and the monks were able to defy their physiological response to cold. They could comfortably sit on a mountain top in the midst of falling snow, dressed in only a loincloth and covered with a sheet. As the snow fell onto their sheets, it melted as they sat in comfortable warmth.

From years of intense prayer and solitude, these holy men were capable of raising their body temperatures through the use of their minds. This is an example of raising their body temperatures through the use of their minds. This is an example of the power of belief; if you believe you can do it, you can do it.

In some tribes, Dr. Benson found the shaman, or the medicine man could point to somebody after being found guilty by his peers in a trial, and say, "Go home and die," and the person would go home and die. Why? because he so strongly believed in the power of the shaman. This is one of many examples of the power of belief.

Remember, if you think you can or you think you can't, you're right.

You will be mentoring others who may believe they are incapable of learning or doing well in school, who may believe they will not be accepted, who may believe the teachers are being unfair to them. Some of what they believe may be true. Your job will be to listen to them and to let them know, from your perspective, how they can use their abilities to fit in and to learn, essentially, to guide them as your beliefs guide you.

The point is your beliefs determine your success or lack of success in life. Think about which beliefs guide you?

Sometimes beliefs have been passed down from one generation to another, and, as a result have a tremendous effect on you. For two summers I taught school administrators in Lithuania with my training partner who goes every year. This country had been under Russian rule for 50 years, a military occupation that devastated their school system; and our job was to work with the administrators in order to have them aware of effective methods used in our country to help raise their education system to current standards.

In Lithuania we encountered some beliefs that are different from what we are used to.

On a hot day, I would open a window and the door in order to get a cross breeze, to help compensate for the lack of air-conditioning in the classroom. As soon as I did this, one of the ladies would immediately get up and close the window or close the door. Being concerned about the comfort of the students, I would again open the window and open the door. Finally, class members would say, "No, no, you can't do that! If you sit in a draft, you will get a cold and possibly die."

They believed this. They believed if they sat in any draft, they would catch a cold. This is a perfect example of the power of belief.

When I first got married, my mother--in--law was horrified that I washed my hair at night and went to bed. She believed I would die, that I would get a cold and die.

Think about what beliefs you have. Jot down some of these things you have learned from your parents and peers. What beliefs do you have about yourself, your background, your abilities, your acceptance, your appearance?

Are your beliefs positive or negative in each area? I always thought I could not go to college because "nice Irish girls did not run away from home." That's what my father said. I believed it, at least for a little time.

Do you believe you're good in math? Do you believe you're good in English? Do you believe you're good in science? Do you believe you're good in physical education? Can you sing? Can you dance? What are your beliefs about yourself physically, mentally, spiritually? Those beliefs often determine your successes and/or failures in life.

All you have to do is change those beliefs by having somebody point out to you what your strengths are. We may know we have them, but having someone we look up to point them out will make a big difference. It's amazing when somebody hits the nail right on the head. You know it; they know it.

In a recent newsletter Martin Rooney, Founder of Training for Warriors, wrote the following to his students: My question for this week warriors is, *"Do you believe you are amazing?"* You might like to say "yes," but I guarantee that in this fast-paced world, perhaps you might have forgotten. I am here to remind you if you don't think you are special, you are dead wrong. You can do anything you put your mind to. Spend enough time working at your dream and anything is possible. Want a degree? Go study. Want a black belt? Hit the mats. Want to lose weight? Clean up your diet. You really are amazing. You just need to believe."

ASSIGNMENT: In your Journal write about the significance of "belief" in your life. Do you have any beliefs that are holding you back from doing what you would like to do? What positive things do you know about yourself? List them all!

CHALLENGE: Be prepared to discuss how your beliefs impact your behavior.

Gail A. Cassidy

PART FOUR

MENTOR TRAINING

Gail A. Cassidy

OVERVIEW OF PART FOUR

To learn about the person you will be mentoring, your teacher will provide you with basic information: name, grade, and the basic challenges the student is facing.

In your first meeting with your mentoree, you can start the conversation by introducing yourself and welcoming him or her by telling them how happy you are for the opportunity to meet and work with him/her.

You can then ask for additional information from the "Workshop For Mentors" pages. This is done in a light, pleasant manner with the understanding they can just use their imaginations about their future.

From their responses to these questions, you will get a better understanding of what they are interested in.

Ask them what they would like to talk about and how you can help them in any way,

Notice that there are no questions about problems they may be facing in their lives. That information will come out in future discussions.

You want them to know that you are there for them.

You may not be able to help them with their math homework, but you can let them know where they can get help. If you are unsure, tell them that and then ask your teacher for recommendations.

Your sessions should be ones where your mentoree feels comfortable and feels as if she/he can trust you.

Gail A. Cassidy

WORKSHEET FOR MENTOREES

(Encourage your Mentoree to keep a Journal for their answers.)

- Right now, what do you must enjoy doing in your spare time?

- Who are your best friends? (Include family members, if appropriate.)

- What is one thing you would change in your life if you could?

WHAT DOES YOUR PERFECT FUTURE LOOK LIKE?

- What would you like to do with your life when you graduate?

- Where would you like two live? Describe your surroundings in detail.

- Who would you like to be there with you?

- What do you do every day?

- How do you look? Feel? (Can you feel the wonderful feelings of success?)

- Do you believe it is possible for your dream to come true?

Remember, if you are the architect, the designer, the author of your life.

Make it a great one!

MENTOR PREPARATION

Mentorees will be asked to complete a preparation form to bring with them every week. No pressure, no grammar checks. This is strictly for their benefit, a record for them to see what they have accomplished since your last session.

If they have accomplished nothing, that is just a "what is;" it's not a judgment. All you want to know is what they accomplished since the last session. By having to write it down and knowing they have to write it down, mentorees are more apt to do it because it is embarrassing not to, especially because you are an upperclassman. They are the ones setting the agenda. They are the ones determining how much they are going to do.

Ask your mentoree, "**What have you accomplished since the last session?**" Suppose they say, "Nothing." Here's an opportunity to learn more about your new friend. Find out why by gently asking, "**Why did you say you wanted to do it, but then decided not to?**" You may uncover information that will be a benefit to your understanding of your mentoree and that you can use to help him. What did not get done, but intended to? What challenges and problems are they having?

In all probability you will run into kids who have backgrounds different from yours. You do not know what is going on their homes. You don't know what is preventing them from accomplishing what they had intended to do.

One student who was, at one time, a great student, suddenly stopped working, developed an attitude, and was always tired. I didn't know why.

> One day I asked her to stop by my classroom after school. I asked her if there was a problem? Her eyes welled up with tears as she told me about her mother in the hospital who was dying (she had AIDS). Because she was the oldest of four children, she was taking care of the other three children with their homework, plus cooking and cleaning plus going to the hospital every night. She had no time of her own. There was not a father in the picture. Aunts and uncles came on occasion, but she was now not only a student, but also a mother and housekeeper and cook.

The line addressing challenges and problems they are facing now, may be more than your mentoree wants to share, and that is fine. If, however, your mentoree has obvious challenges, encourage him to write it down.

Also encourage them write down what the opportunities that are available to them, opportunities such as the possibility of getting a teacher who will work with them on their math or their English or their science or their spelling, or whatever it is?

Ask, "Are you aware of what could be done to make life a little bit better?" These are things that you can discuss with your guidance counselor if you are not sure.

You are not responsible for getting their grades up. You may not be good in math yourself. Either way, you are not going to be the one that helps them in subject matter areas, but you could direct them to someone who could. If in doubt, ask your advisor for advice.

The mentoree is filling this out. He gets to determine what he wants to work on today. He determines the agenda. You just go along and, again, in a safe atmosphere where you accept them and validate them in any way you can.

Initially, they may be there with reluctance, but as you get them talking and learn more about them, they will come to recognize that you can be of help to them, if only by being a friend to them.

Finally, ask your mentoree to write what they promise to do by the next meeting. Because it is his call, he will make the decision regarding his own intentions, ensuring a greater chance of compliance. If you keep track of these forms, hopefully you and your mentoree will see a progression as well as what effect you are having on them.

MENTORING PREPARATION FORM

What I have accomplished since our last session:

What I did not get done, but intended to:

The challenges and problems I'm facing now:

Opportunities that are available to me right now:

I want to work with my mentor during this call on:

What I promise to do by the next call:

Additional Notes:

Signature_____Date

Gail A. Cassidy

HOW TO PREPARE FOR YOUR MENTORING SESSION

NOTES SHOULD BE KEPT FOR YOUR MENTOREE

Before each session

- **REVIEW YOUR NOTES**.
- Ask yourself, "What do I believe this mentoree most needs help with?"
- Encourage your mentor to be prompt. Start on time always.

DURING SESSIONS

SESSION ONE:

- Discuss the Worksheet for Mentorees and them complete it, either now or at home.
- Go over the mentoree's Workshop responses. Discuss each area and have your mentoree decide on the area she most needs to work on in order to feel progress toward her goal.
- Review and get commitment on the need for the Mentoring Preparation Form to be filled out each week.
- Go over page on **"Format of Things to Talk About With Your Mentor."**
- Request your mentoree to start thinking about **"10 Goals to Reach in the Next 90 Days"** although no action needs to be taken on this form at this time.
- Review to **"Things to Talk About With Your Mentoree."**
- Ask your mentoree to start to think about what she is tolerating and begin the list.
- Work together on the first Mentoring Preparation Form for the next meeting.
- It is important for the mentoree to understand the benefits of working with a mentor. If necessary, refer to the "15 Benefits of Working With a Mentor."
- By the end of the *first meeting*, you and your mentoree should have a clear set of agreed-upon expectations, insofar as what he is expected to do in preparation for each week's meeting. In addition, make sure the mentoree has the Mentoring Preparation Form, Values Sheets, and Toleration list.

SESSION TWO:

- Review each of the items on the Mentoring Preparation Form.
- Check to see which values the mentoree has selected.
- The values chosen may represent the "needs" of your mentoree. For example, it may be important that they be admired, be encouraged, have freedom, have fun, have prestige, etc.

- Discuss Tolerations.

  (Remember the section on Tolerations: Tolerations are what you put up with. What stress or restrictions do you have in your environment? Are there things that you are tolerating that you don't want to? What is your mentoree tolerating, and how is that affecting his or her behavior?)

- Get commitment for date, time, and "things to do" for next week. Remind mentoree to complete Mentoring Preparation Form.

SESSION THREE:

- Review each of the items on the Mentoring Preparation Form.
- Discuss tolerations. This is a good time to see where stress has lessened or increased.
- Assign **"10 Goals to Reach in the Next 90 Days."**
- Encourage your mentoree to write specific goals **(See S.M.A.R.T GOALS).**
- Mentoring Preparation Form has to be completed for next week and mentoree is encouraged to continue working on his goals and toleration list.
- During the *third meeting,* inquire about the following areas:

  - How are we doing so far?
  - How do you feel about the way we have started? What concerns do you have at this point?
  - Are there any areas you feel uncomfortable about?

- By the end of the *third meeting,* your mentoree should have his goals outlined and be working on an action plan to reach **"10 Goals To Reach in the Next 90 days."**

SESSION FOUR:

- At the end of the *fourth meeting,* your mentoree should have an action plan fairly well developed and, after considering your input and suggestions, be ready to launch his action plan.
- Begin to be on the lookout for any obstacles.

Hopefully, you will have at least a semester to work with
your mentoree. A year would be even better.

ASSESSMENT

Becoming aware of mentoree challenges prepares you for the course of action you may recommend your mentoree pursue. Knowing the areas she needs to work on gives you the opportunity to make your meetings more meaningful and productive.

It is recommended you keep this Assessment Sheet inside your mentoree's folder, rating the behavior of your mentoree on a monthly basis, as you see her, using the following scale:

A. **Always demonstrates this behavior**
B. **Often demonstrates this behavior**
C. **Infrequently/never demonstrates this behavior**
D. **Not applicable**

BEHAVIORS

1. Demonstrates strong will to succeed.
2. Is passionate about his work.
3. Is willing to make personal sacrifices to get the job.
4. Overcomes obstacles.
5. Is tenacious.
6. Is open and receptive to constructive feedback.
7. Maintains a positive attitude, even in times of adversity.
8. Shows trustworthiness.
9. Handles change well.
10. Works well under pressure.
11. Controls emotions, even in stressful times.
12. Has short- and long-term goals.
13. Has an action plan to achieve goals and objectives.
14. Sets high standards of performance for self.
15. Is reliable and on time for work.
16. Is a good listener.
17. Communicates well with others.
18. Is approachable.
19. Shares information with others.
20. Treats others fairly and with respect.
21. Maintains confidentiality.
22. Displays personal integrity.
23. Shows sincerity.
24. Shows promise of success.

CAUTIONS:

- If your mentoree is not completing his work, be alert to problems in his life, which he may not be discussing.
- Your mentoree may tend to dominate the session by distracting you with crises, complimenting you on something you said or just chatting.
- Your job is to keep the discussion on track for the greatest benefit of your mentoree. (An aside: having had a personal trainer, I quickly became adept at keeping him talking for the entire hour, the result being I didn't have to do any hated exercise. Who won? Who lost?)

GENERAL INFORMATION:

- Challenge your mentoree but don't push. Encourage small steps.
- Set expectations and praise each step forward, each step completed.
- There is no such thing as "should," they "should" have done it or "should" not have done it. They can't do what they didn't do, so there is no way they could have "should" it.
- Discuss any of the following during sessions:

• something great that happened	• failure
• a problem	• the past
• an upset	• the future
• an insight	• fears
• a breakthrough	• new ideas
• a dilemma	• financial challenges
• a complaint	• financial solutions
• a promise	• contributions made
• feelings	• progress
• growth	• setbacks
• relationships	• advice
• possibilities	• feedback
• life planning	• decisions
• success	

Gail A. Cassidy

S.M.A.R.T. GOALS

- **Specific**
- **Measurable**
- **Action Planned**
- **Results Oriented**
- **Time Phased**

GOAL SETTING

An effective way to get what you want in life is to set goals. When you set a goal, you make a commitment to be accountable for your actions. As a mentor who sets goals, you are in a good position to encourage your mentorees to do the same.

Getting your mentoree to set goals is the best way to get him or her accountable for what they say they want to do.

Encourage your mentorees to set goals, specifically **S.M.A.R.T. goals.**

S is Specific: "I want to increase my English grade by 10 points by the end of the marking period."

M is for Measurable" "Improve by 10 points." It is action planned, the "how" are you going to do that? And it is results--oriented when you add, "I want to increase my English grade point by 10 points, by handing in all of my work on time.

A is for Action Planned. "I will hand in my papers on time." It's action that has been planned. They know what action has to be taken in order to improve the grade.

R is Results Oriented. "Handing in all of my work on time will increase my grade." They know and understand what will result is they follow their plan.

T is for Time Phased. "I will increase my English grade by December 1st." It is very specific, and it is measurable.

Practice for yourself; set goals that are S.M.A.R.T goals.

Challenge your mentorees to set ten goals to reach in the next 90 days. Encourage them to select only goals they want to accomplish and only in the areas they desire.

When they or you set the right goals for yourself, you should feel excited and a little nervous, ready and willing to go for it. Make sure they and you include the benefits they anticipate by reaching their goals.

POTENTIAL AREAS FOR GOAL SETTING

GRADES

INCOME

MAKING FRIENDS

SOCIAL ACTIVITIES

SIBLING RELATIONSHIPS

TEACHER RELATIONSHIPS

PARENTAL RELATIONSHIPS

GROOMING

JOB

SPORTS

HOBBIES

ENVIRONMENT

SUBJECT MASTERY

ATTITUDE

Gail A. Cassidy

10 GOALS TO REACH IN
THE NEXT 90 DAYS

Select only goals you want to accomplish and in the areas you desire. When you set the right goals for yourself, you should feel excited, a little nervous, ready and willing to go for it! **INCLUDE BENEFITS YOU ANTICIPATE**.

ENVIRONMENT

PERSONAL WELL-BEING

MENTAL WELL-BEING

RELATIONSHIPS

VOCATION/CAREER/FINANCE

THINGS TO TALK ABOUT

How we feel about ourselves has an influence on how we live our lives and how we interact with others—our peers, teachers, family members, friends.

Rather than directly asking, "How are you feeling about yourself?" you could ask, "How do you feel about your classes, your classmates, your teachers."

Try to elicit specific instances of why they feel as they do. For example, if they state that a teacher is picking on them in math class, ask them to tell you more about that. You may find that math is particularly challenging to them, and here is where you can suggest getting extra help or talking to their guidance counselor about help available.

You could ask, "What do you want to do when you graduate?"

The answer to this question could give you the information you need to better understand how they are viewing their lives.

Attitudes toward their classmates, teachers, friends, and family will usually come through when they talk about their experiences in school.

Remember, your primary goals are 1) to keep them in school and 2) help them recognize what is special about themselves and 3) encourage them to do well in school.

"What has occurred since our last meeting?" opens up an opportunity for you to learn how your mentoree spends his/her days. You may ask, **"What's the best thing that has happened since we last met?"** and build on that, encouraging more of the same.

By asking about **"breakthroughs"** and **"insights,"** you are encouraging awareness in your mentoree. By focusing on those two words, you are also directing them toward a positive response.

"New choices or decisions" lets them know that they are in control. They do have a choice in life; they can react as they choose to react. That's freedom! Asking about **"Relationships"** may give you information you could use to better understand your mentoree.

You can also refer to your **Placemat Charts summarizing the course, "Specific Things to Talk About,"** to find additional ways to learn more about your mentoree and find ways to change their attitudes about school, if they have a negative attitude.

The first one, **"Progress on goals, projects, activities?"** is included in order to give your mentoree a sense of responsibility. He chose the goals; therefore, he has the responsibility to work on the selection.

Gail A. Cassidy

"What have you done that you are proud of?" allows the mentoree to brag a little and feel good about his progress.

"What resistance are you encountering?" may elicit information that would be of help to you to better understand your mentoree's challenges.

The rest of the questions are self-explanatory. This is not a prescription; the questions are here in order to help "reach" your mentoree, to get your mentoree talking, and to assure the mentoree that you are a supporter, that you understand, and that you have no judgment. Remember, these questions are all located on the Summary Chart at the beginning.

Remember S.A.V.E: Safety, Acceptance, Validation, and Enthusiasm. They do work, and they will make a huge difference in the lives of whomever you work with.

As you are working with your mentor, you can occasionally ask one of the **"Wants"** questions, which are also listed on the Summary Sheets at the beginning of the book.

"WANTS"

- Where do you want to live – to work?
- How do you want to look, to feel, to sound?
- What do you want to do every day?
- How much do you want to earn each year?
- What kind of relationship do you desire to have with your family, your friends?
- What obstacles do you see keeping you from doing what you want to do In life?
- How can I help you succeed?

Most teens do not know specifically where they want to work, but they may have a preference for indoor or outdoor work. They may know if they would like to work indoors in a hospital, a bank, a museum, hotel, studio, restaurant or outdoors in construction, landscaping, sports, travel, etc.

Getting them talking about possibilities plants the seed in their minds about the future and their place in it.

Be aware that you have these questions in reserve in the event you are met with silence during your mentoring sessions. Asking any of these questions and then answering from your perspective may encourage your mentoree to open up to you.

Use your discretion and ask what you are comfortable asking. Eventually, once you are totally comfortable, you will find the list unnecessary.

"INTERESTS"

- What do you feel strongly about? What really upsets you on TV news?
- Whom do you admire and why?
- What characteristics do they have that you share or would like to have?
- What places make you feel good? (smells, noises, feeling)
- What do you enjoy doing in your spare time?

An easy way to find a topic of conversation is to find out what your mentoree feels strongly about: politics, women's issues, education reform, SAT's, sports, justice, college, foods, space exploration, texting, freedom of speech, rules, school, and so much more.

Audience members at talk shows who may be shy are not shy when a topic they feel strongly about is introduced.

When you ask **"Whom do you admire and why?"** it is **the "why" that is revealing**. Is it the sports figure or the sports figure's talent and ability that they admire. It is a family member; if so, what about the family member do they admire—their honesty, humor, integrity, talent. **The "why's" tell you what is important to your mentoree.**

"Places that make you feel good" is fun. I love the smell of a school (I was a teacher) and my daughter loves the smell of a pool (she was a world-class swimmer). Smells evoke memories—good and bad.

What places make you feel safe? As a child, I would love to go to the airport to watch the planes take off and land—long before I was ever a passenger, and I still love airports.

"What do you enjoy doing in your spare time?" relates to what drives your mentoree, what is meaningful, what he/she cares about. From this response, you know what not to waste time talking about.

All of these questions are ones you would use without conscious thought when meeting a new friend. Here they are more purposeful because you want to make sure your mentoree feels safe with you (acceptance) and that what he/she likes is okay, which is form of validation. The enthusiasm is a natural result of a great conversation.

Initially, you may be as uncomfortable as your mentoree. That's fine!

"MORE INTERESTS"

- **What magazines do you read?**
- **What articles?**
- **What books?**
- **What makes you feel special? (past achievements, honors, recognitions, hobbies?)**

Gail A. Cassidy

- **What would your perfect day look like?**
- **If you can dream it, you can be it.**
- **What do you dream or daydream about?**
- **What do you NEED to make you happy?**
- **List 10 things you would do if you were a billionaire.**

What difference does magazine choices make? If you were flying to New Zealand, you would want something to make the time go faster, and a magazine is a perfect choice. The one you select is indicative of what interests you. I would not purchase a sports or automotive magazine, and you may not choose to buy *O*, Oprah's magazine.

There is not a right or wrong; there are just preferences. What your mentoree chooses may give you added information you could use to help him/her.

I was teaching a class of young executives and asked them to bring in an item for which they had received recognition in their past. I was very surprised to see that six of these grown men had brought in their Pinewood Derby cars from their elementary school days. I have had people bring in A+ papers from elementary school or a newspaper article featuring something they had done. One brought in a pen he had won in a speaking contest. Perhaps your mentoree has something he/she values from earlier years.

Whatever it is, it is a clue as to what the mentorees values.

A "Perfect Day" response could include location—town, state, country, home, hour of awakening, people there, friends, morning routine, activities throughout the day, evening plans, bedtime hour—anything that would make a perfect day.

We all **daydream** to some extent. If your mentoree cares to share the types of daydreams he/she has, you will find they probably fit into his "perfect day."

Do you know what you need to be happy? Family, friends, good grades, acceptance, love, gratitude? The list is endless and individual!

The **"10 things you would do if you were a billionaire"** is a fun exercise— the making a "bucket list" at an early age.

Do remember, **the primary goal of mentoring is not only to keep students from dropping out of school, but also to achieve each student's highest potential according to his or her aptitudes and dreams.**

The goal is not to mold a mentoree to be like us or his teachers or friends; it is to be the best that your mentoree can be.

Your challenge may be to avoid judgment. Remember the first human relation principle: Do not criticize, condemn, or complain—perhaps the toughest of them all.

REMINDER: Every human being has the basic needs, no matter what their age, and that is **to know they're lovable and to know they're worthwhile.** When you are working with a mentoree, if they feel those two things----to know they're lovable and to know they're worthwhile—they are going to blossom; they're going to do well.

The next section includes different ways to run your mentoring sessions,

Gail A. Cassidy

ADDITIONAL SUGGESTIONS FOR MEETINGS

HOW ARE YOU?

- How you are feeling about yourself - good stuff and bad stuff?
- How you are looking at your life?
- How you are feeling about others?

WHAT HAS HAPPENED SINCE OUR LAST CALL?

- What has occurred to you since the last call?
- Any breakthroughs and insights?
- Any new choices or decisions made?
- Personal news?

WHAT ARE YOU WORKING ON?

- What progress have you made on your goals, projects and activities?
- What have you done that you are proud of?
- What you are coming up against?

HOW I CAN HELP?

- Can I explain something about which you are unclear?
- Can I provide you with more information?
- Do you need help developing a plan of action?
- May I offer you a strategy or advice?

WHAT IS NEXT?

- What is the next goal or project you want to take on?
- What do you want for yourself next?

(From Coaching Forms Book, 4th Ed., Devby Thomas Leonard, Coach University)

QUESTIONS TO ASK WHEN CONVERSATION SLOWS DOWN

On the next few pages, you will find a number of questions you could ask your mentoree. Read these questions beforehand and decide which ones would be most appropriate to ask your mentoree.

- Is there an area of our work together that you would like to spend more time on?
- Tell me three ways that our working together is helping you get to where you desire to go?
- What goals have you made the most progress in?
- How has our working together improved your personal relationships?
- At the end of this year together, where do you want to be
  - Career-wise?
  - Financially?
  - Physically?
  - Socially?
  - Spiritually?
  - Mentally?
- What personality traits do you feel you have improved on?
- What do you feel most grateful for in your life?
- What would you most like to contribute to the world?
- What do you feel your purpose in life is?
- What are you most proud of having accomplished at this point in your life?
- If you could have five habits ingrained in you that would improve your life, what would they be?
- What do you see as the greatest opportunity available to you right now?
- How are you going to take advantage of that opportunity?

EVEN MORE IDEAS FOR QUESTIONING

Go through this list of questions and check off only those questions that you would be comfortable asking.

- What do you want? What are you afraid of? What is this costing you?
- What are you attached to? What is the dream?
- What is the essence of the dream? What is beyond this problem?
- What is ahead?
- What are you building towards?
- What has to happen for you to feel successful?
- What gift are you not being responsible for? What are your healthy sources of energy? What stops you?
- What's stopping you? What's in your way?
- What would make the biggest difference here? What are you going to do?
- What do you like to do?
- What can I do to make you happy right now?
- What do you hope to accomplish by having that conversation?
- What do you hope to accomplish by doing that? What's the first step?
- What's important about that?
- What would it take for you to treat yourself like your best friend? What benefit/payoff is there is the present situation?
- What do you expect to have happen? What's the ideal?
- What's the ideal outcome? What would it look like?
- What's the truth? What's the right action?
- What are you going to do? What's working for you?
- What would you do differently?
- What decision would you make from a place of abundance? What other choices do you have?
- What do you really, really want? What if there were no limits?
- What aren't you telling me that's keeping me from helping you?
- What needs to be said that has not been said?
- What are you not saying?
- What else do you have to say about that?
- What is left to do to have this be complete?
- What do you have invested in continuing to do it this way? What is that?
- What comes first?
- What consequence are you avoiding?
- What is the value you received from this conversation?
- What is motivating you? What gets you hooked? What is missing here?
- What does that remind you of? What do you suggest?
- What is underneath that?

- What part of what I said was useful? And how so? What is this person contributing to the quality of our life? What is it that you are denying yourself right now?
- What do you need to put in place to accomplish this?
- What is the simplest solution here?
- What would help you know I support you completely? What happened?
- What are you avoiding?
- What is the worst that could happen? What are you committed to?
- What is your vision for yourself and the people around you? What don't you want?
- What if you knew?
- What's your heart telling you?
- What are you willing to give up?
- What might you have done differently? What are you not facing?
- What does this feeling remind you of?
- What would you do differently if you tapped into your own wisdom? What does your soul say?

(Laura Berman Fortgang, *Living Your Best Life*)

Gail A. Cassidy

CHALLENGES FOR YOUR MENTOREE:

Mark Twain once said, "I can teach anybody how to get what they want out of life. The problem is I can't find anybody who can tell me what they want."

Hopefully your mentorees have an idea of what they want. To challenge them further, on a separate sheet of paper, complete the following:

- Create a list of 12 things you want in your life.
- Make a list of 12 things you DO NOT want in your life. (Check Tolerations sheet)
- Schedule at least 3 hours over the next week to think carefully (and take notes) about what you truly want in the years ahead.
  - In one year_____
  - In five years_____
  - In ten years_____
  - In twenty years_____
- Make a list of what you need in life
  - In one year_____
  - In five years_____
  - In ten years_____
  - In twenty years_____

- Make a list of the blocks or challenges that you see as standing in the way of where you want to be.
- Create a list of 100 people you know. Even if you are still in school, look at the different professions that exist. One of them may at some time appeal to you, such as artist, plumber, doctor, lawyer, teacher, minister, etc.

Look at this list and see if there is someone on it who could help advance your career or give you a lead.

How could a plumber advance your career if you choose to be a bookkeeper? They may need a bookkeeper too. Everyone is a potential client for someone good with numbers.

Most jobs are found through people who know somebody who is looking for an employee. It is possible that your plumber could recommend to the chiropractor, whose pipes he just fixed, that he hire you.

Networking is invaluable in finding a job and in finding clients for a business. You want to build a base that can help you and that you someday can help in return. Prepare your list slowly. There is no rush, and be prepared to update the list as necessary.

**THESE ACTIVITIES ARE FOR THOSE MENTOREES
WHO ARE READY FOR THESE CHALLENGES.**

MENTOR AWARENESS

BE ALERT!

A mentor is someone who has a positive impact on the lives of others, someone who sees more talent, ability, and "specialness" within their mentoree, than the mentoree sees in herself, and someone who helps bring out these special traits and characteristics.

Please understand that as a student mentor, you are not trained nor are you equipped to deal with medical and/or mental illnesses, alcoholism and/or drug addiction. If you suspect a problem, you should notify the appropriate person (teacher or guidance counselor).

All information obtained in connection with mentoring activities is considered confidential. Conversations and observations made regarding the mentoree and/or the mentoree's family will be held in confidence.

The exceptions to this confidentiality statement include concerns that the following harm may occur or is currently occurring:

1. *Physical, sexual or emotional abuse*
2. *Suicide*
3. *Illegal weapons*
4. *Substance abuse*
5. *Danger to self and/or others*

Again, in the above-mentioned instances, you, as the mentor, are obligated to **bring the concerns to the attention of the appropriate authorities or school personnel.**

From Greek mythology the riddle that Oedipus answered when he reached the Sphinx is applicable to mentorees.

"What walks on four legs in the morning, two legs at noon, and three legs in the evening?"

This riddle is associated with man. Four legs relate to crawling as a baby (the morning of our lives), two legs for walking at noon (the middle part of our lives), and three legs in the evening (our twilight years) referring to legs plus a cane. A mentor is similar to a third leg for someone who, at this point in his life, cannot stand alone.

The person being mentored, the mentoree, decides the direction, the speed, the route, the environment, the degree of intensity; and the mentor supports each step she takes.

Gail A. Cassidy

The mentor encourages the best direction, the appropriate speed, the best route, the best environment, and the appropriate degree of intensity. By the end of a year's mentoring, hopefully your mentoree will be able to successfully take her place and walk alone without the aid of a cane.

> **ASSIGNMENT: In your Journal, write your reactions to Mentor Awareness and how you feel about reporting what you see or experience with your mentoree.**

7 HABITS OF HIGHLY INEFFECTIVE MENTORS

This is want you do not want to be!

- Start from the point of view that you--from your vast experience and broader prospective--know better than the mentoree what's in her best interests.
- Be determined to share your wisdom with them--whether they want it or not; remind them frequently how much they still have to learn.
- Make sure they understand how trivial their concerns are compared to the weighty issues you have to deal with.
- Remind the mentoree how fortunate he is to have your undivided attention.
- Neither show nor admit any personal weaknesses; expect to be their role model in all aspects of career development and personal values.
- Demonstrate how important and well connected you are by sharing confidential information you don't need (or want) to know. Discourage any signs of levity or humor--this is a serious business and should be treated as such.

**ASSIGNMENT: Meet in small groups and talk how
you would like a mentor to be with you.**

Gail A. Cassidy

MISCELLANEOUS

- Stress to mentorees that the power to transform their lives comes from them.
- Eliminate the following from mentorees' vocabulary: **"If only," "yes, but," "should have," "could have,"** and other words that will hold them back or give them an excuse.
- **HABITS:** What was learned can be unlearned. Habits take approximately 21 days of uninterrupted practice to take hold. Have mentoree select desirable new habit(s) and keep a record to see how long it takes to implement.
- The key to happiness isn't what you're doing; it's what you are getting out of what you are doing.
- A rich person isn't the person who has the most; it is the person who needs the least.
- You don't find happiness; you release it.

"Success is getting what you want. Happiness is wanting what you have." -Dale Carnegie

REVIEW

This entire section on Mentor Training contains considerable options when working with your mentoree.

The Mentoring Preparation Form is the form you will work with most often. Assessments, goals, SMART goals, goals to reach in 90 days are options.

The list of things to talk about with your mentee is exhaustive in order to give you, the mentor, options.

Choose what you will be comfortable talking about and asking about.

Mentoring will be as much a growth opportunity for you as it is for your mentoree.

Mastering the sections on People Skills, Questioning and Listening Skills and understanding the impact of Tolerations and Beliefs will benefit you in your interactions with everyone you know.

PART FIVE

PRACTICE SESSIONS

CASE STUDIES

**Before we begin our Case Studies, divide into small groups.
Assign one topic per group. Present results to the class.**

- Why is it important that we have a mentoring program here?
- We want to keep kids in school, but how?
- We want to prepare them for good citizenship, but how?
- We want to teach them self-value; we want to motivate them; we want to provide a safe haven to grow and to learn; and we want to give them life--enhancing skills, but how?
- How do you develop character, provide hope, provide opportunity, provide security?
- And what impact would this have on the school if all students were mentored, if all kids felt safe?

Logic dictates that mentorees' grades should go up. A better atmosphere would be a natural repercussion. The positive results would impact the school and the town. Long-range, the graduates, the students you mentored, are the ones, along with you, who will impact the country. Wouldn't it be nice to be an active part of this positive experience!

How can these positive outcomes be accomplished? With practice! In this session, you will be able to practice the skills you have learned. Working with a partner, you apply the mentoring techniques you have learned. Repetition is what will make these skills a part of you.

You might call this session a practicum because you will have an opportunity to actually practice with a partner. The first thing you're going to do is pair off with a partner and decide who initially is going to be the mentor and who's going to play the role of the mentoree.

You will be presented with a number of scenarios from which you can choose. The mentoree will read the scenario and act out the part, but will not tell the mentor which scenario was chosen.

Mentors: You hold a session and be prepared to report the positives learned and the negatives encountered.

Each mentor will teach the class what he learned.

Switch positions and repeat the process---- the mentor will become the mentoree and visa-versa.

In addition to creating your own scenarios, possible scenarios could include problems regarding the following:

- Problems at home
- Dislike of school
- Math challenges

- Fear
- Lack of acceptance
- Teacher problems
- Bullying

DIRECTIONS:

- Pair off with partner
- Decide who is mentor and who is mentoree
- **Mentoree:** read the scenario to yourself (don't share) and act out the part
- **Mentor:** hold a mentoring session and be prepared to report A) positives learned B) negatives encountered
- Each mentor teaches class; switch positions and repeat process.
- Choose one of these scenarios after you've decided who's going to be the mentoree. Do not tell your mentor which one you chose; just act out the problem as you, the mentoree. Take time and then come back when you're all finished.

SCENARIOS: (Teacher: Cut scenarios into strips, fold, and have mentoree choose at random.)

- **Everybody picks on me. I hate school.**

- **I can't get math, never could, and I hate it, so why should I stay in school?**

- **Anybody gets in my way and I'm gonna punch them out. I can take care of myself.**

- **Teachers don't care. They just get their paycheck and show up. Why should I care?**

- **Kids bully me for no reason.**

- I just feel depressed all the time.

- My brother ran away.

- I smoke pot.

- I'm in trouble with the police for stealing.

- I think I may be gay.

- I have to help my mom. She lost her job and I have younger brothers and sister who have to eat, so I can't hang around here.

- I don't need school. I'm going into the Army.

- School is like a total waste of time. Nobody cares, and everybody picks on me.

Gail A. Cassidy

- I don't have to take any "stuff" from my teachers. I'll punch them out if they give me a problem.

- School is boring!!

- My dad lost his job, and I have to get a job to help support the family.

- My mom had a nervous breakdown and is in the hospital.

- Why waste time in school when I'm never going to use math or history?

- I'm just stupid. I can't get it and I don't care.

- Who are you to tell me what to do? I don't have to listen to you.

- Man, you gotta know, I just don't care. I'm just waiting till I'm old enough to quit!

- I'm sick of being picked on. I'm afraid to even use the boys' room.

- I hate going to gym class where everyone makes fun of me. Forget it!

- I am sick and tired of having to study, then fail my chemistry tests.

Add suggestions from the students of possible scenarios,

We have switched roles. The mentor has been the mentoree and vice-versa, so you have all had an opportunity to practice.

If you have enough time, keep practicing; keep switching partners. The first couple of times may feel uncomfortable, especially in this class because you know one another. When you are working with mentorees, they are younger and will likely be looking up to you and perhaps a little scared. The experience is different when you are actually working with the younger students.

REVIEW

Kids mentoring kids: the mentorees want acceptance and belonging; they want validation; they want self-esteem.

The mentors can fulfill those "wants" by using the human relation principles.

To review:

Ice Statue: Accept people as they are.

Cheerleader: Be enthusiastic in all you do.

Headphones: Listen. It is the greatest compliment you can pay someone.

Bubbles: Thoughts. Change your thoughts and you change your world. -Emerson.

Thermostat: You can't control what happens to you, but you can always control your reactions.

Praying hands: Accept what is, e.g., Serenity Prayer.

Candy bar: Treat others as you wish to be treated.

C: Do not criticize other people. No one ever appreciates it.

+ sign: Look for the positives in everyone.

You will also have the self-satisfaction of making a difference in the lives of the students you work with, your mentorees.

An additional benefit you will experience is the positive impact on your self-concept. That alone can be adequate justification for participating in this mentoring program.

Keep in mind what Mother Theresa said, "**There is more hunger for love and appreciation in this world than there is for bread.**"

Another thing to keep in mind along with the human relation principles is The Code of Ethics:

- Show respect to get respect
- Be nonjudgmental
- Seek the strengths of each mentoree
- Provide a safe atmosphere

- Know you cannot NOT communicate
- Set high expectations
- Make sincerity your number one priority
- Be sensitive
- Set boundaries
- Have fun
- Smile, and
- Be enthusiastic

Most of all, remember the acronym **S-A-V-E. It** sums up everything you've learned.

S - **Safe atmosphere**, no bullying, no putting down, no teasing.
A - Total **Acceptance**.
V - **Validation**, find their strengths.
E - And do this all **Enthusiastically**, and you will find that this may be one of the greatest adventures you've ever undertaken.

Good luck and, again, thank you for participating.

For additional information on books and seminars available, go to <ins>https:// www.cassidycoursescom</ins> and click on the books and seminar tabs

PART SIX

MENTORING PROGRAM ORIGINS

OVERVIEW OF PART FIVE

Wanting to know more about a subject begins somewhere by an event or experience in your life that stays with you and enhances awareness.

My initial motivation to solve a problem I saw as solvable was the students I worked with who were not high achievers but had the ability to be very good students.

Why they didn't work up to their capacity puzzled me until I started listening to student essays on their perceptions of the world. Observing the reaction of their peers was heart-warming.

The results astonished me. Peer reactions had far greater impact on the students than adult reactions. Kids understood kids; that was the beginning of Kids Mentoring Kids. The acceptance and validation of their peers changed students in very positive ways.

My basic belief in the importance of acceptance and validation led me to the development of the Code of Ethics already covered.

The next step was to develop a program for Kids to Mentor Kids. My initial target audiences were high school kids in inner city areas, kids I was hoping to keep from quitting school. Meetings for this after-school program were cancelled a few times because of drive-by shootings and once, a murder in the park—events this group of teenagers were exposed to on a daily basis.

The next section shows sample student reactions to one another.

Gail A. Cassidy

MENTOR PROGRAM ORIGINS

You now know why mentors are so important in the world today, and you know how to conduct mentoring sessions. You will have an even deeper understanding of your mentorees when you read the next three chapters.

How a person thinks, the level of his self-esteem, his choice of values, and his practice of good interpersonal skills are major determinants of a person's achievement and satisfaction in life. These intangible components of success can be developed in mentorees through a successful mentoring relationship.

The above-mentioned concepts are difficult to teach, but they can be acquired by mentorees through the skillful guidance of a mentor. The sincerity of a mentor's response to the actions and accomplishments of his mentoree is the recognition and validation that will directly affect how a mentoree thinks, his level of self-esteem, his values, and his interpersonal skills.

The mastery of the **Mentor's Code of Ethics** by the mentor ensures that each mentoree will be able to ultimately internalize the components of success; namely, learning how to control his thoughts, increase his self-esteem, choose positive values, and practice good interpersonal skills.

THOUGHTS

The first success component relates to **THOUGHTS**. A little-recognized ingredient for success is how a person thinks!

"Change your thoughts and you change your world."

As stated by philosopher Marcus Aurelius, "A man's life is what his thoughts make of it."

> Today this concept regarding the importance of thought would be called *The Secret or the Law of Attraction.* The Bible reinforces this concept where it is written *"What* you sow, so shall you reap." If you plant radishes, you cannot expect to pick cucumbers. If you think negative thoughts, you attract negativity into your life. Your life is what your thoughts make it to be.

A major goal of mentoring is to have mentorees rise to the challenge and accept responsibility for their lives, starting with developing an awareness of their thoughts and how it is they who control their own thoughts.

Their actions come from their thoughts; therefore, they can control their actions. That is a huge concept to "get," and it is an invaluable one. This insight is also valuable for a mentor to possess.

In order for mentorees to succeed, they have to believe that they are capable of doing what they want to do in life, and they have to believe that they are worthy of believing in themselves. They can find the work they were meant to do; and when they listen to themselves and follow their own wisdom, they will find that meaningful work.

I was pleased that the mentors felt free to agree and disagree with some of the points I was making. To me, this was the beginning of critical thinking, a thought process you want your mentorees to develop.

For example, one young man disagreed with the premise that "work is something you were undoubtedly meant to do."

> He said, "I do not agree with this, because I think that some people do not need to work to be happy or to make them feel good. Your ultimate goal should be to find what you love to do and become an expert at it."

> He explained his response by saying, "There are people out there that are making all the money in the world, and they are the most unhappy people because they hate what they do."

> He substantiated his point by giving an example. "There is a kid I work with at the local golf club who is twenty-four and he used to work on Wall Street, but he left that and now he is an assistant pro there making less money, but he said he is much happier because he is doing what he likes."

Students, both mentors and mentorees, are encouraged to find their true vocational uniqueness, utilize each day, develop a plan, set goals, cash in on their mistakes, visualize, dream, and take responsibility for their attitudes.

Hopefully, your mentorees are at the stage of life where they are ready to believe in themselves, especially when they have an authority figure (a student in a higher grade) who believes in them. Here is where a mentor is invaluable as someone who can get his mentoree to not only understand that beliefs and attitudes determine how a person performs, but also can encourage them to change negative beliefs to positive beliefs.

> The statement, "the past does not control your future" was a relief for one student who wrote, "I'm glad to learn that my past does not have to control my future. This basically tells us that we have a chance to learn from our mistakes. The way that I look at it is that everyone has numerous chances to rebuild their lives and learn from mistakes that we all make."

> Another student, a bright young man, was in agreement. He felt "it was a statement to live your life by." He recognized that people are responsible for finding their own uniqueness. His decision to look into mechanical engineering for next year is a

Gail A. Cassidy

quantum leap forward for him. He certainly is capable. Until this year, however, he did not believe that he was; and that belief was created by his thoughts.

Another student, on the other hand, was more realistic in his assessment and stated numerous examples of how he saw reality; namely, "you have to do what you have to do in life in order to make a living." Having come from overseas as a youngster, he is very aware that his father works hard to make a living in America, support his family, and keep his son in private school.

One student wrote, "I accept that there is a sleeping giant inside of me. Once you begin your wishful thinking, the giant begins to awaken." This is how we want our mentorees to feel.

Through their written papers, I could also discern aspects of a student's character.

For example, one student did not believe you had to do anything in life that benefits others. "I can see helping yourself, but what if your dream has nothing to do with helping others?"

Another student stated, "I find it hard to trust in my self-reliance and to trust my decisions. I think someday that I will be working somewhere, and I will not love what I am doing."

Although I see this young man as a bright, charismatic person, his self-assessment is much less positive.

What was encouraging to me about the students' reactions was their ability to see beyond the words, to relate it to themselves and their experiences and the experiences of their family members, and to be able to have within their grasp the knowledge that they are in charge of their lives. That knowledge alone is wonderfully empowering, and it is something new for most of these students. They were personally validated by the words of the author.

"Every man carries in his eye the exact indication of his rank." –Ralph Waldo Emerson

Your mirror shows you the person others see when they look at you, and you can fashion yourself into any kind of person you would like them to see. If you act the part, you will become the part.

In their essays, students had to write about

1) what they wanted seen when people looked at them and
2) how they are going to enable people to see that.

The purpose of the exercise was to reinforce the concept that they have to believe in themselves before others will. They are the authors of their existence.

Sharing this information with mentors is your gift to them, but first you want to apply it to yourself.

Many students said how they want to be seen, i.e., funny, considerate, caring, pretty, and nice, among numerous other adjectives. Most then went further; for example, desiring to be seen "as the type of person that they can always come and talk to."

Even more, however, students began to realize that if they act a certain way, they would become a certain way, akin to Shakespeare's previously mentioned wisdom, "Assume a virtue if you have it not."

> A female student, who averaged 75 in most of her subjects until this year, wrote, "I learned that you could do anything you want to as long as you believe and strive. Anything is possible if you really push yourself."

> Today her average is 15 points higher than it was just last year. Her motivation this year is that she believes in herself and in her abilities. She now knows she can perform better and she does.

> One shy young man wrote, "You can make yourself into any kind of person. All you have to do is act the part and you will become the part." He related this belief to how he acts at work where he has to be outgoing, in contrast to the shy image he projects at school.

> From another student, "This summary has been very influential in my life. It has affected me in a positive way. If you put yourself in the right or positive frame of mind, you can do anything you put your mind to."

> I was pleased that by-and-large, the class was able to read beyond the mirror image in the directions. They were able to relate the messages being taught to sports, grades, careers, and friendships.

There is power in the internalization of the belief, "If you act the part, you will become the part." The members of this class, in particular, need to realize that they can affect their own futures, that they have the power to be the person they desire to be, and that the responsibility is on them to be that person.

To keep the messages constantly in front of the students, I encouraged them to find and post motivational messages and poems on their mirrors and walls as constant reminders of the importance of believing in yourself.

One suggested reminder is as follows:

- **I BELIEVE IN MYSELF**
- There is no one better to be than myself.
- I am enough.
- I get better every single day.
- I am an amazing person.

135

Gail A. Cassidy

- All of my problems have solutions.
- Today I am a leader.

> You're divinely designed And perfectly made for the work of mankind. This truth you must cling to through danger and pain. The heights man has reached you can also attain. Believe to the very last hour, for it's true. That whatever you will, you've been gifted to do. (by Walter Doyle Staples, *Think Like a Winner!*).

> *"The man who does not read books has no advantage over the man who cannot read them."* -Mark Twain.

> *"You are not what you think you are, but what you think, you are."* Norman Vincent Peale.

As a mentor, you can continually remind your mentoree to find and post positive messages on the walls, in notebooks, on separate sheets of paper or any place where they can be reminded of the message. The motivational sayings emphasize how essential the belief in themselves is.

Mentoring, which takes place in a safe, sincere atmosphere, is a place where mentorees are recognized as important people with valid feelings, where they are totally accepted and not judged, and where their beliefs and attitudes are validated by their mentor, reinforces that vital belief. Hopefully, the messages will sink in.

The following are sample positive affirmations from https://www.thepathway2success. com/101-positive-affirmations-for-kids

- I get better each and every single day.
- I am an amazing person.
- All of my problems have solutions.
- Today I am a leader.
- I forgive myself for my mistakes.
- My challenges help me grow.
- I am perfect exactly as I am.
- My mistakes help me learn and grow.
- Today is going to be a great day.
- I have courage and confidence.
- I can control my own happiness.
- I have people who love and respect me.
- I stand up for what I believe in.
- I believe in my goals and dreams.
- It's okay not to know everything.
- Today I choose to think positive.
- I can get through anything.
- I can do anything I put my mind to.

- I give myself permission to make choices.
- I can do better next time.
- I have everything I need right now.
- I am capable of so much.
- I believe in myself.
- I am proud of myself.
- I deserve to be happy.
- I am free to make my own choices.
- I deserve to be loved.
- I can make a difference.
- Today I choose to be confident.
- I am in charge of my life.
- I have the power to make my dreams true.
- I believe in myself and my abilities.
- Good things are going to come to me.
- I matter.
- My confidence grows when I step outside of my comfort zone.
- My positive thoughts create positive feelings.
- Today I will walk through my fears.
- I am open and ready to learn.
- Every day is a fresh start.
- If I fall, I will get back up again.
- I am whole.
- I only compare myself to myself.
- I can do anything.
- It is enough to do my best.
- I can be anything I want to be.
- I accept who I am.
- Today is going to be an awesome day.
- It's okay to make mistakes.
- I am making the right choices.
- I surround myself with positive people.
- I am a product of my decisions.
- I am strong and determined.
- Today is going to be my day.
- I have inner beauty.
- I have inner strength.
- No matter how hard it is, I can do it.
- I can live in the moment.
- I start with a positive mindset.
- Anything is possible.
- I radiate positive energy.
- Wonderful things are going to happen to me.

- I can take deep breaths.
- With every breath, I feel stronger.
- I am an original.
- I deserve all good things.
- My success is just around the corner.
- I give myself permission to make mistakes.
- I am thankful for today.
- I strive to do my best every day.
- I'm going to push through.
- I've got this.
- I can take it one step at a time.
- I'm working at my own pace.
- I'm going to take a chance.
- Today I am going to shine.
- I am going to get through this.
- I'm choosing to have an amazing day.
- I am in control of my emotions.
- My possibilities are endless.
- I am calm and relaxed.
- I am working on myself.
- I'm prepared to succeed.
- I am beautiful inside and out.
- Everything is fine.
- My voice matters.
- I accept myself for who I am.
- I am building my future.
- I choose to think positively.
- I am becoming the best version of myself.
- Today I will spread positivity.
- The more I let it go, the better I will feel.

Choose five to focus on and change whenever you desire.

REFERENCES

If you believe that this book will liberate you, then you are already a victim of your own illusions before you even start reading. You and only you must decide to take these suggestions and turn them into constructive, self-fulfilling behaviors. - Wayne Dyer

The books used in the preparation of this book fall into five categories: (1) Personal philosophy books, (2) Validating informational and Implementation books and articles, (3) Teaching methodology books, (4) Research methodology books, and (5) Education research books.

(1) My personal philosophy found its roots many years ago in the most influential book I have ever read on raising or teaching children; namely, *Your Child's Self-Esteem* by Dorothy Corkhill Briggs.

Her philosophy created for me a strong set of beliefs that has permeated all of my dealings with children, my own and others.

(2) It is a philosophy later substantiated through my readings of authors such as Wayne Dyer, Robert Fulghrum, Richard and Linda Eyre, Napoleon Hill, Depak Chopra, Denis Waitley, Ken Kragen, Barbara Sher, Stephen Covey, Les Brown, Ken Blanchard, Og Mandino, Anthony Robbins, Dale Carnegie, Norman Vincent Peale, Dan Millman, Claude Bristol, Robert Shuller, and others whose names I have forgotten. The newest names added to my list are Rosenblatt and Pradl.

I attempt to use the basic principles as espoused in these books when working with students and/or mentorees, especially with the "unmotivated" group. They have been made wrong so many times, they expect to be considered wrong. Studies indicate that the most important factor [for a child's self-esteem] seems to be the degree of warmth experienced by the child, rather than any particular techniques of child training (Louise Rosenblatt, *Literature As Exploration*). Warmth is an integral part of making a person feel important.

(3) The third category, Teaching Ideas, is headed by Janet Allen's wonderful book, *It's Never Too Late: Leading ADOLESCENTS to Lifelong Literacy.* This highly motivated teacher believes that students will become readers when they are allowed time and given the support to read. She touched on areas I could definitely relate to with my Writing Lab students. When I was discouraged, I would reread the underlined sections of her book.

I frequently referred to "E.I. or emotional intelligence" when I spoke to my students who feel their I.Q. or intelligence quotient is below par. Helping me understand this relatively new concept are three books: *Emotional Intelligence* by Daniel Goleman, *Emotional Intelligence at Work* by Hendrie Weisinger, and *Measuring Emotional Intelligence* by Steve and John Simmons. The last book, in particular, is very helpful in understanding and presenting the concept.

Gail A. Cassidy

Other, more main-stream books which I found informative were Gini Graham Scott's *The Empowered Mind*, Rick Pitinos' *Success is a Choice*, Brian Tracy's *Maximum Achievement*, plus books such as *A Whack on the Side of the Head* by Roger von Oech, Joel Saltzman's *If You Can Talk, You Can Write*, *Writing Out Loud* by Jefferson Bates and Michael Gelb's *Mind Mapping: How to Liberate Your Natural Genius*. The last book is a great example of brainstorming on paper.

(4) Category Four, **Research Methodology**, consists of *Seeing for Ourselves: Case-study Research by Teachers of Writing* by Glenda Bissex, *Writing to Grow: Keeping a Personal-Professional Journal* by Mary Louise Holly, and *The Art of Classroom Inquiry* by Ruth Shagoury Hubbard and Brenda Miller Power.

(5) Category Five, **Educational Research,** includes books such as *An Unquiet Pedagogy* by Eleanor Kutz and Haphzibah Roskelly, a book I found controversial in parts. David Berliner and Bruce Biddle's *The Manufactured Crisis* and Miles Meyers' *Changing Our Minds, Negotiating English and Literacy* are books everyone in the education field should read. They are both motivating and eye-opening as is Regie Routman's *Literacy at the Crossroads In Defense of Elitism* by William Henry makes the reader think as does David Kearns and Denis Doyle's *Winning the Brain Race.*

Although I have not mentioned all of the books that I read in preparation for this book, I have covered those that stand out in my mind. Reading these books became similar to eating potato chips. I couldn't stop at just one.

WORKS CITED AND CONSULTED

Allen, Jane. It's Never Too Late: Leading ADOLESCENTS To Lifelong Literacy, Portsmouth: Heinemann.

Anthony, Dr. Robert. Doing What You Love, Loving What You Do. New York: Berkeley Books.

Berliner, David C. and Bruce J. Biddle. The Manufactured Crisis. NY: Longman.

Bristol, Claude, The Magic of Believing. New York: Cornerstone Library.

Briggs, Dorothy Corkille. Your Child's Self-Esteem. New York: Double Day.

Cassidy, Gail. Literature for Democracy "Response." Martha's Vineyard.

Covey, Stephen. The Seven Habits of Highly Effective People. Free Press.

Dyer, Wayne. Erroneous Zones. New York: Funk and Wagnalls. Fortgang, Laura Berman. Living Your Best Life. Tarcher.

Goleman, Daniel. Emotional Intelligence. New York: Bantam.

Grabhorn, Lynn. Excuse Me, Your Life is Waiting. Hampton Roads Publishing Company.

Kearns, D. and D. Doyle. Winning the Brain Race. San Francisco: ICS Press

Leonard, Thomas. The Portable Coach. New York.

Scribner, Myers, Miles. Changing Our Minds, Negotiating English and Literacy Illinois: National Council of Teachers of English.

Rosenblatt, Louise M. Literature as Exploration. New York: The Modern Language Association of America

Staples, Walter Doyle. Think Like a Winner! New York: Pelican.

APPENDIX A

ADDITIONAL COURSES TO ENSURE ACCEPTANCE AND VALIDATION

Gail A. Cassidy

TWO ADDITIONAL COURSES TO ENSURE ACCEPTANCE AND VALIDATION

Our retired teacher, Abby, will tell you about two additional courses that have positive impacts on their participants.

Abby is well aware of the ineffectiveness of "telling" people to be kind or enthusiastic or nonjudgmental or any of the Human Nature Laws.

She is well aware that if a student doesn't feel she is worthwhile or lovable, she may find it difficult to be kind to others, especially those who have been unkind to her. He might be challenged to be enthusiastic. That's human nature.

The change has to come from within, not from being "told" how to act, but to experience the desire to accept and act on the Laws of Human Nature.

What is important to kids? And to all people?

If the goal is to have every child believe in him or herself, whose validation is most important to them? Abby thought about that and remembered a story she had read many years ago that impacted her at the time and is timeless and significant even today.

That memory motivated Abby to develop the first course, a program where every student will be validated by their peers every time they speak. That course is called "Speaking Skills for Teens." (https://www.cassidycourses.com)

The second course is about them. When Abby started teaching at VoTech, she had written a book on teaching English to disinterested students. It bombed. The next week, she brought in copies of the Manual for a book she had written years ago, *Discover Your Passion*. It was an immediate hit! Why? Because it was about them. The exercises recognized what is special about each person, so Abby taught English through *Discover Your Passion For Teens*.

Because of her concern about high school dropouts, Abby had developed a program called *Kids Mentoring Kids*. Upper grades students mentor lower grade students. This, of course, is what you just completed.

That is what the following three programs do, including this Kids Mentoring Kids Program.

1. They provide the experience of helping younger students who look up to them as a result.
2. They learn the basic human relation skills through teaching them to underclassmen.
3. They learn the importance of listening, a skill that extends far beyond the classroom.
4. They experience the problems of others and through helping them, are able to solve many of their own problems.

Gail A. Cassidy

COURSE #1 - SPEAKING FOR TEENS

After Abby was satisfied with her Laws of Human Nature as applied to students, she thought long and hard about how to implement the concepts in a realistic and enjoyable manner. The first major challenges Abby confronted were timing and "buy-in" from students and the administration. How could she convince teachers and administrators that self-esteem, communication skills, and human relation skills are worth spending time on where there is no way to empirically measure their progress?

Abby believes that every child should be exposed to ways to maximize their skills and abilities. What vehicle could she develop that would teach and demonstrate respect for one another and be recognized as something of value by school administrators?

She started with one course that she considered to be a no-fail course, a course that would assure acceptance among a diverse group of kids, engender a belief in oneself, and would be an opportunity to experience all 13 Human Nature Laws.

With 180 days of school a year, divided into 36 weeks or 18 weeks a semester, Abby designed her first course, a 14-course (allowing a couple of weeks of leeway time including vacations and holidays) that would enable students to find the best in their peers while learning a skill and putting all 13 Human Nature Laws into practice.

As mentioned previously, Abby was motivated to develop a course that incorporated acceptance and validation on a daily basis. She made her decision after reading the touching story of teacher, **Sister Helen P. Mrosla** writing about a student in the first third grade class she had taught at Saint Mary's School in Morris, Minnesota. The young man, Mark Edlund, lost his life in Vietnam. When his special effects were returned to his parents, they found a yellowed, crisply folded paper in his wallet. He had carried it with him since 7th grade. That one day so many years ago, his teacher asked the class to write the names of every student in class on the left side of the paper. She then asked them to write one good thing about that person next to their name. That weekend, she took everyone's lists and made each student a copy of all of the good things their classmates had written about them. Mark Edlund had kept that paper with him all of these years as had many of his classmates who attended his funeral.

This story is significant because of the impact those words had on this young man and his classmates. These weeks will have a similar impact on you. At the end of the course, each student will receive all of the positive comments from fellow students about every talk he or she had given.

Google "Mark Eklund" to read his entire story. It was a game-changer for Abby. His story reinforced her belief that everyone needs to feel accepted and validated in order to experience a happy, satisfying life.

Although Abby had read this story many years ago, it always stayed in her mind. Mark's teacher had implemented a simple act of acceptance and validation wrapped up in a list, a list that impacted each individual in the class. Abby pondered on how to replicate this in a meaningful, relevant, fun manner.

After many months of work, Abby produced her 14-week course called "Speaking for Teens." In addition to learning speaking skills—openings, evidence, closings, body language, and attitude training, Abby added a "list-type" of activity.

Every student had a card with his or her name at the top and an assigned number (it's easier to find numbers than alphabetized names). If there are 25 students in the class, each student writes his or her name on 25 cards along with the number. The cards are then dispersed among the other students, so every member has a complete packet to cards for every other classmate.

On the wall is a chart listing three areas students are to comment on after each person speaks: the talk itself, the delivery of the talk, the audience reaction to the talk. The one caveat is **ONLY POSITIVES** can be written on the cards—absolutely no negative comments.

As each student goes to the front of the room, he/she gives the teacher a sheet of paper with the first line and the last line of the talk. After the talk, the teacher asks for two comments from class members, again, only positives.

The teacher adds one more positive, then on the student's paper, writes 1) a positive comment, 2) an area of improvement comment, and 3) another positive statement. The students' grades are dependent on how well they address the "area of improvement" comment.

The impact of this course proved to be the most satisfying of Abby's entire career. She has over 19 pages of testimonials from kids who used their experience in the class when applying to college or for a job. A brief sampling includes: (The entire 19 pages can be found at https://bit.ly/2Mkflgc). Here are examples of what students wrote upon completion of the course.

CONFIDENCE

- First speech: "I was sweating and shaking. I was nervous to get in front of the class. I then felt better when my classmates clapped for me when I was going up. I felt a little better, but I was still nervous. When I finished my talk my classmates clapped for me and said I did a good job. I also felt better because they were quiet, and they listened to my talk."
- "I gained more confidence when talking in front of an audience."
- "Then I present a show of my own, hear positive comments from my classmates and feel good about myself. I still don't want to be a center of attention but now I'm more comfortable doing what I have to do."
- "Public Speaking is the best class I have ever taken. I saw the change in people like C and S who were never outspoken and the change in them is incredible. I learned more about my image."

- "I feel I have gotten a lot out of this course. I am confident when speaking in front of a group of people (especially my peers). I know I can get through an interview successfully. In saying all this, it comes as an obvious statement when I say I thoroughly enjoyed this course."
- "As a result of this course, I have gained a confidence before my audience that I have never felt before."
- "I have learned a lot from it because my confidence has grown and now I can't wait to give my next speech."
- "This class has made a big difference in my life. Before Effective Speaking I was a lot shyer than I am now, a couple of months later. The first time I went to make a talk, I was scared to death. I was worried about what the rest of the class would think. Now I feel so comfortable talking in front of people. I actually have a lot more fun giving the talks now that I have overcome my fear."

Abby was pleased with the results of the *Speaking Skills for Teens* course, a one-semester elective. She believed the next important aspect of a high school student's training should be in the area of finding their passion or purpose in life. See *Discover Your Passion for Kids* next.

(Training videos course available at https://www.cassidycourses.com)

COURSE #2: "DISCOVER YOUR PASSION FOR TEENS"

In the Speaking Skills for Teens course, the Laws of Human Nature were addressed. The second part of what Abby determined to be needed for high school students is direction. This course is an 8-week elective, preferably for juniors. Every student is special, and this course zeros in on what makes each one special and how that knowledge can help them plan their futures.

Computerized aptitude tests are frequently used to determine careers in which students may be successful. *Discover Your Passion* takes a different approach. On a computerized test, a student must choose one answer, e.g. your favorite color. If their favorite color isn't listed, the test is skewed, albeit ever so slightly.

With the exercises in *Discover Your Passion,* students are asked questions they can discuss with their peers, and there are never any wrong answers. These sessions are opportunities for insightful thinking for each student taking this elective.

Abby pondered a number of questions unrelated to her academic schedule. She thought, "Wouldn't it be nice if everyone could do what they wanted to do every day and still earn money? How great would it be to feel excited when you awaken every morning? Wouldn't everyone like to feel that what they do makes a difference in the world?"

Abby believes all of this is possible once a person knows what their passion is and knows how to put that passion to work. Master motivator and author, Barbara Sher, says it best in the title of her book, *I Would Do What I Love If Only I Knew What It Was.*

By the last session of this elective, Abby's experience is that students will know not only what their passion is but also how to earn money pursuing that passion whether it is full-time or as an income-producing hobby.

Abby recognizes that no two people are alike. Everyone has unique talents, knowledge, skills, and abilities. Finding which skill, which bit of knowledge, or which talent a person most enjoys using will lead to discovering their passion.

Two of Abby's favorite people concur. Wayne Dyer says, "There is no scarcity of opportunity to make a living at what you love; there's only a scarcity of resolve to make it happen. Even Oprah says, "Your job is to discover what your true calling is." Therein lies your happiness.

Abby developed *Discover Your Passion* as a course to help students discover their passion and earn money doing what they love. The four major objectives of this program are

(1) to help them clarify their passion,

(2) to prepare them for a job search or help some of the students to find their business,

(3) to familiarize them with marketing basics, and

(4) to help them learn how to make their dreams come true. Students can progress at their own rate or work in small groups.

She created major lesson divisions according to the information regarding the topic. Some sessions will take longer than others. Her experience is that students enjoy the journey, whether they are headed to college or to a vocational school to master a skill or to go out and find a job.

Abby designed the program to allow each participant to recognize what is special about themselves and to find a direction in life. The information students glean from their responses are important pieces necessary to complete their jigsaw passion puzzle. Fit them all together and they will have their passion.

THE IMPORTANCE OF HAVING A PURPOSE

Another book that impacted Abby is *Man's Search for Meaning,* where Victor Frankl tells of his horror-filled days as a prisoner in a Nazi prison camp. He said he made an interesting observation about those people who survived the terror and hardships of their ordeals.

He stated, in effect, that those who had a purpose in life survived; those who did not see any hope or believe they a purpose, died, even if physiologically equal. That is a significant observation.

Similarly, Wayne Dyer in *Real Magic* recalls the words of the prison inmate, "Nothing is more likely to help a person overcome or endure troubles than the consciousness of having a task in life."

Alter his words a bit by using the word *passion* in place of *task,* Abby read *"Nothing is more likely to help a person overcome or endure troubles than the consciousness of having a passion in life."* She believes that that is what teachers want students to uncover as they progress through this course.

The #1 deadly fear of many people is having lived a meaningless life. Abby's husband started his own business many years ago, because, as he said, he didn't want to wake up on his deathbed and say to himself, "I should have given it a shot."

"The only courage you ever need is the courage to live your heart's desire." -Oprah

Now is the time!!! This elective is the way!!!

In her e-zine, Barbara Sher, author of *Wishcraft,* wrote
"You're all obligated to do what you love because that's where
your gifts lie and those gifts belong to all of us."

Implicit in that statement are three premises:

1. everyone is here for a purpose, and
2. everyone is here to help others, and
3. gravitating toward pleasure, e.g., doing what you love, is not only okay, it is mandatory if you want to help others and if you are seeking the wonderful illusives called happiness, satisfaction, and serenity.

That reminds Abby of her favorite quote "The time to be happy is now; the place to be happy is here, and the way to be happy is by helping others." - Charles Englehardt. That says it all.

Abby strongly believes that now that they are in high school, the time has come for students to discover how to use their gifts to make the world a better place. She believes that doing so will not only enrich their lives but also the lives of others. This is an opportunity to make the world a better place.

Having defined the baker's dozen of essential human nature laws, Abby got busy working on ways to implement what she felt was important to work on in order to motivate kids to learn and to be their best selves. She knew she couldn't just tell others to show respect to get respect, be non-judgmental, etc. She needed a way for kids to experience these laws and hopefully adopt them.

Over the next few years, Abby worked on the development of these three separate courses that would show rather than tell the laws of human nature with the intent of having them "buy in."

She started with Mindset or Belief and integrated the concepts into the three courses but devoted one course, "Discover Your Passion for Teens," as the opportunity for teens to study themselves without judgment and make decisions based on what they experienced in the course.

The importance of belief! Napoleon Hill wrote in his book *Think and Grow Rich*: "What the mind can see and believe, it can achieve." Abby believes the concept is still the same; it's still true -- if a student's mind can think up or conceive of an idea and believe in it, he can achieve it.

Abby continues: "If you believe you can do something, what's stopping you? What have you gotten to believe that acts as an obstacle to your success? Do you believe you can't "get" math, you can't make friends, you aren't bright, you can't sing, you are clumsy, etc." Some may be true, and that's fine. The point is, if you believe it, you act accordingly.

"If your mind can conceive and believe in doing something, you can achieve it. If you believe you can, what's stopping you? What have you gotten to believe that acts as an obstacle to your success?"

One of Abby's favorite sayings that she repeats in every course is from Henry Ford, the founder of Ford motors and the first assembly line for the manufacture of cars. He said, "If you think you can or you think you can't, you're right."

Frequently kids, especially "at risk" kids believe they're incapable in some manner, who believe they're not accepted, who believe the teachers are being unfair to them. Some of their beliefs might be true, but they must be listened to and encouraged."

The point is," according to Abby, "our beliefs determine our success or lack of success in life. Kids need to know they are worthwhile, that they have something to offer the world. Everybody does, but sometimes talent is just not utilized because a person doesn't believe in the existence of that talent.

Our beliefs guide us as it does our students.

What beliefs do you, the reader, have about yourself, about your background? Are they positive or negative?

What about your abilities? Do you believe you're good in math? Do you believe you're good in English? Do you believe you're good in science? Do you believe you're good in phys. ed.? Can you sing? Can you dance? What are your beliefs about yourself physically, mentally, spiritually? Those beliefs determine how you do in life.

And, of course, Abby believes the easy answer is: all you have to do is change those negative beliefs or have somebody point out to you what your strengths are. It's amazing when somebody hits the nail right on the head. You know it; they know it.

Every person has strengths and weaknesses. In this course, "Discover Your Passion for Teens," Abby has exercises that enable each student to find theirs; and, along the way, may find their life's work. There are no wrong answers!

COURSE #3: "KIDS MENTORING KIDS"

(The Purpose of This Course)

Having taught in one capacity or another for decades, Abby finds her heart goes out to those kids who "fall between the cracks," the potential dropouts. It is for that reason that she developed the two programs already mentioned, both of which are enriching and fun. They are validating of each participant; they provide direction, and they teach communication skills, including human relations skills which translates immediately to improved civility among classmates.

Finally, it came to her: why not use the remaining quarter of the year, as an elective, to train kids to mentor other kids—juniors mentoring incoming freshmen. This is the course you now own.

Initially, Abby designed the mentoring programs for the students who needed help, whether academically or socially. To her great surprise, she found that those who benefitted most from the mentoring experience were the mentors.

Statements such as "I felt important," "It was the first time I felt looked up to," "I like the fact that I can be trusted and that I can help someone else," "I know that I need someone to talk to sometimes—being there for someone else is great," "I've learned that I can be a bigger person, a person to go to in a time of trouble," and "I loved helping the underclassmen" were typical of the responses she got on follow-up of the programs.

The responses from parents of those being mentored were also positive. One mother said told Abby that because of his mentor, her son actually looks forward to going to school. Before that, he was scared to leave his home. Teachers commented on improved grades of those being mentored. It's all good!

Abby believes we have to keep in mind one important question: What do gangs have to offer "disaffected" kids? They offer acceptance. She believes we can do better than that. She believes that Kids Mentoring Kids can promote acceptance/validation in a safe environment, in the schools.

How can that be done? Experiencing what it is like to help another person, to make a difference in the life of that person, is more impactful than words could relate. That is what this program is about.

There are kids who are not at risk as well who could use a mentor to help them achieve their goals. This course shows them how.

Kids trained as mentors can have a positive impact on the lives of others. They can see more talent, ability, and "specialness" within their mentoree than those not paying attention can.

Gail A. Cassidy

As previously stated, the evaluations came as a total surprise. The mentors were more frequently the benefactors. They said things such as, "I loved being a mentor because no one had ever looked up to me before. I felt important. I felt respected." You can't teach those things; you can only experience them. That's why Kids Mentoring Kids is so important to have in every school.

Abby believes that students need to be encouraged to start acting as they desire to be, and they need to know they can be whatever they desire, one step at a time. The capacity for creating the life they want resides within each of them.

Being a mentor means showing acceptance and guidance to someone who needs your support. Your reward is the tremendous satisfaction awaiting you as you watch your mentorees grow and develop into the people they desire to be.

By the end of a year's mentoring, hopefully each mentoree will be able to successfully take her place and walk alone without the aid of a mentor.

Abby emphasizes that in order to maximize their potential, *mentorees first must feel they are safe, accepted, and respected as they are.* What helps to instill this feeling is constantly seeing the invisible tattoo on their foreheads, which reads, "Please make me feel important." In other words, "Don't criticize me or make me feel like a loser."

It is a mentor's job to help mentorees move through phase three, *Social-Acceptance* and phase four, *Self-Esteem*, in order to facilitate their reaching the highest level, Five, *Self-Actualization*. This final phase puts the mentoree in a position to make a difference in the world.

Abby states that in one way or another, people young and old will gravitate toward someone who provides a source of validation. Validation is a human need, and this is where being a mentor comes into play. This is their opportunity to help mentorees experience acceptance and validation.

Overcoming years of negativity and poor results may be the greatest challenge for those who are unmotivated. While mentorees' improvement may not be vast, their improvement is possible by moving in small increments toward a higher level of proficiency in their job skills and their interpersonal skills.

APPENDIX B

TIPS BOOKLET:

"HOW TO BE THE BEST THAT YOU CAN BE"

TIPS ON HOW TO BE THE BEST THAT YOU CAN BE

LIVE THE BEST LIFE YOU CAN BY BEING THE BEST YOU CAN BE

How can you make your life better than it is now? Hopefully, some of the tips in this section will help you live a happier life, especially in your dealings with other people; but first, as mentioned previously in this book, there are three things you need for yourself. You need food--wholesome and nutritious--to nourish your body. You need shelter--a safe place to live. You need support--someone to let you know you are important to the world.

When you have these three essentials: food, shelter, and support in your life, you can work on making a difference in the world by positively influencing and impacting the lives of other people. But first, you have to train yourself to FEEL GOOD EVERY DAY. The following chart summaries what is necessary for you to FEEL GOOD EVERY DAY, everyone's ultimate goal.

YOUR PHYSICAL WELL BEING REQUIRES
SOUND NUTRITION AND DAILY EXERCISE

YOUR MENTAL WELL BEING REQUIRES Always Looking For
Gratitude and Beauty every day and practicing daily Meditation/Reflection

Everyone's Ultimate Goal is to feel good!!

To Feel Good, <u>Choose</u> and Experience Any of These "FEEL GOOD" EMOTIONS:

Passion, Bliss, Happiness Reverence, Joy Trust, Optimism Inspiration Harmony Appreciation

Most importantly, every day express GRATITUDE and seek BEAUTY, Validate everyone, look for their positives, and show everyone you meet kindness, appreciation, and respect.

THOUGHTS ARE CHOICES and can be either POSITIVE OR NEGATIVE--you make the choice!

TO FEEL BAD, CHOOSE EITHER JUDGMENT and/or NEGATIVITY through feelings of Revenge, Excuses Procrastination, Anger Justification, Gossip Hate, Ill Will, Blame Sickness, Gloom, Despair Criticism, Hatred, Restrictions, Anxiety, Fear, Shame.

THESE FEELINGS EQUAL DEPRESSION, SADNESS, e.g., "I DON'T FEEL GOOD"

The nice thing is, you have the power and ability to choose to feel good or to feel bad every moment of every day. Choose I FEEL GOOD!

Gail A. Cassidy

The following tips will help you as you interact with others. Human nature is the same all over the world, and these tips reflect the basics of human relations. Making these tips a part of you will help you be more effective in working with others and will help you maximize your own potential.

Enjoy every day of your life. Each one holds a surprise for you. Look for that surprise each day, and, when you find it, write it down, keep it forever, and see the beauty in whatever occurs.

GENERAL PHILOSOPHY OF LIVING

1. • See the invisible tattoo on everyone's forehead that reads: "**PLEASE MAKE ME FEEL IMPORTANT.**"
2. • Find at least one happening in each day to be grateful for.
3. • Look for positives in every person.
4. • Recognize the specialness of diversity.
5. • Provide an atmosphere conducive to happiness, e.g. a smile on your face, comfort, simplicity, etc.
6. • Vary your daily activities. Do something different that will revitalize you.
7. • Remember, humans of any age need breaks.
8. • Know that everyone you meet has something special to offer.
9. • Living in the moment is where you find happiness.
10. • Learn the Serenity Prayer: "God, grant me the serenity to accept the things I cannot change, courage to change the things I can and the wisdom to know the difference."
11. • "See" and/or "feel" your positive day before you climb out of bed. Use positive self-talk.
12. • Be (or act) enthusiastic about everything you do. It's contagious; it carries over to the people in your life.
13. • Accept people as they are, and then provide the atmosphere for them be happy and grow.
14. • Learn from every person you meet, every friend.
15. • Ask yourself, "Does it really matter?"
16. • Being right does not always work, e.g.,
    Here lies the body of William Jay, who died maintaining his right of way. He was right, dead right as he sped along, but he's just as dead as if he were wrong.
17. • **HAVE FUN!**

ATTITUDE

18. • Park your ego at the door; it hinders relationships with friends and family.
19. • Give your friends and people you know a reason to check their negative attitudes at the door also.
20. • Know that people "mirror" you. They reflect what they see, hear, and feel from you.
21. • Shake things up. Make changes. "If you always do what you have always done, you'll always get what you've always got."
22. • Show people through your own example what fun having a great attitude is.
23. • Be patient.

24. • Positive attitudes are catching, wherever you are.
25. • Show respect to get respect.
26. • Know that attitude is a choice everyone makes every day.
27. • Explain that people cannot help what happens to them, but they are **always** in charge of their responses.
28. • Remember, there is a pause between stimulus and response. Choose your response carefully.
29. • Ask yourself why you are **choosing** to be unhappy, bored, tired, sad, happy.
30. • Know that attitude is the steering mechanism of the brain. Body language can lead to attitude, and vice versa.
31. • Practice changing your attitude by sitting or standing straight, with your head up and a smile on your face. It does work!
32. • Know that it is the attitude of our hearts and minds that shape who we are, how we live, and how we treat others.
33. • Help friends and people you know to recognize their specialness.
34. • Success is feeling good about yourself every single day. That is attitude.
35. • Know and share with the people you know that true power is knowing that you can control your attitude at all times.

HUMAN RELATIONS

36. • Treat everyone as if he or she were your friend's best friend.
37. • Never talk down to anyone.
38. • Find what is special about every person you meet.
39. • **SMILE**. It warms a room.
40. • Use tact when responding to a challenging person. The rewards outweigh "being right."
41. • Know that it is not okay for people to feel your negativity. That is your choice.
42. • Be 100% fair at all times--no exceptions.
43. • Keep in mind that perception is reality--yours and your friends' and the people you know.
44. • Treat every person as you wish to be treated.
45. • Understand that no one **wants** to be wrong.
46. • **Everyone desperately wants to feel special.**
47. • Remember that people gravitate toward people and things that are pleasurable and avoid people and things that are painful. Make learning pleasurable.
48. • **LISTENING** is the greatest compliment.
49. • Try to understand before being understood.
50. • Show genuine appreciation to people you interact with.
51. • Begin corrective action with sincere and honest recognition of what has been done correctly.
52. • Never embarrass anyone. Allow the person to save face.
53. • Use encouragement. Make the error seem easy to correct.
54. • Don't be afraid to admit your mistakes. It will make you appear more human.
55   • Show respect for every person's opinion.

56. • Challenge people to be the best that they can be.
57. • Make **SINCERITY** your No. 1 priority.

COMMUNICATION

58. • Set standards in your everyday life and share them with the people you know.
59. • Know the purpose and importance of what you are doing.
60. • Set high expectations.
61. • Know that 55% of all messages comes from the body. Notice how you can tell your special someone is in a bad mood without any words being spoken.
62. • Know that 38% of the message comes from the voice: inflection, intonation, pitch, speed, e.g., "I didn't say he stole the exam." Seven words--seven meanings.
63. • Know that you **cannot** <u>**NOT**</u> communicate.
64. • Recognize that we don't all see the same thing when looking at the same thing.
65. • Know also that we don't all hear the same things even when listening to the same words.
66. • Control your thoughts; your feelings come from your thoughts; therefore, you can also control your feelings! Choice is control.
67. • Take responsibility for what you say and how you say it.
68. • Listen for the message, yet know that body language can be interpreted as only a clue to the meaning of the message, e.g., arms crossed in front of chest could mean the person is blocking you or could mean the person is actually cold or comfortable.
69. • Learn to lead rather than to try and overcome resistance.
70. • Communicate your enthusiasm through your body and voice.
71. • "One who is too insistent on his own views, find few to agree with him." -Lao-Tzu
72. • Speak with a warm heart.

SELF ESTEEM

73. • Know that a person with high self-esteem does not need to find fault with others.
74. • Remember that people find fault with others when they feel threatened, consciously or unconsciously.
75. • Know that self-esteem is not noisy conceit. It is a quiet sense of self- respect, a feeling of self-worth. Conceit is whitewash to cover low self- esteem.
76. • Remember, people have two basic needs: to know they are **lovable** and **worthwhile**.
77. • Remember, it is a person's feeling about being respected or not respected that affects how s/he will behave and perform.
78. • Helping people build their self-concept is key to being a good friend.
79. • Know that your words have power to affect a person's self-esteem.
80. • Each person values himself to the degree s/he has been valued.
81. • Words are less important in their effect on self-esteem than the judgment(s) that accompany them.
82. • The attitude of others toward a person's capacities are more important than his possession of particular traits.

83. • Bragging people are asking for positive reflections.
84. • Masks are worn to hide the "worthless me."
85. • Low self-esteem is tied to impossible demands on the self.
86. • A person's own self-acceptance frees him or her to focus on others, unencumbered by inner needs.
87. • The single most important ingredient in a nurturing relationship is honesty.
88. • Ask this: "If I were to treat my friends as I treat those closest to me, how many friends would I have left?"
89. • Avoid mixed messages. Be clear in your statements of expectations.

BOUNDARIES

90. • Tolerate no disrespect.
91. • Be consistent in enforcing rules.
92. • Set boundaries.
93. • Find opportunities for others to improve the quality of their work.
94. • Differentiate between the action and the person.
95. • Uncover and address, when possible, the reasons for the person's poor performance.
96. • Make sure people you work with have the skills to succeed.
97. • Focus, as often as possible, on what is right rather than what is wrong.
98. • Give plenty of recognition for the unique gifts of each person.
99. • Keep in mind that you have power in the present moment to change your thoughts, feelings, and attitude about the past.
100. • Take control of your life by focusing on the present.
101. • Remove the word "try" from your vocabulary. "Try" to pick up a pencil. Either you do or you don't.
102. • Find the lesson or value in unacceptable situations.
103. • Know that you have choices in spite of your past experiences.
104. • Turn problems into a learning opportunity.
105. • Have a clear vision of where you are going.
106. • Approach problematic situations with relaxed confidence.
107. • Respond thoughtfully to challenging and/or problem situations.
108. • Avoid making judgments.
109. • Learn problem solving:
     State the problem
     Look for cause or causes of the problem
     Brainstorm solutions
     Choose the best one
110. • Always see beyond your own point of view.
111. • Encourage habits of thought conducive to growth in understanding others, to think outside the box.
112. • Recognize that there is no one interpretation of a situation.

Gail A. Cassidy

LIFE'S TREASURE TIPS

113. • Begin to be now what you will be hereafter. Repetition is the mother of skill.
114. • Know that you too are special.
115. • Enjoy each day and each moment of life.
116. • Make corrections by citing two positives for every negative.
117. • Live in the present.
118. • Be alert for moments of gratitude.
119. • Show lively enthusiasm!
120. • Create an atmosphere of fun.
121. • Build on successes.
122. • Create a routine with varied activities.
123. • Turn on to learning.
124. • Visualize doing well.
125. • Be relaxed.
126. • Make everyone feel important.
127. • Remember, you are what you choose today.
128. • Give yourself opportunities to succeed.
129. • Provide a safe atmosphere--physically and mentally.
130. • Validate yourself frequently.
131. • Your reality is what you make it to be.
132. • Polish your people skills.
133. • Hone your communications skills.
134. • Take excellent care of yourself.

MORE TIPS

135. • Work towards feeling good about yourself. It is man's highest goal.
136. • Always do what you feel is right or true.
137. • Your actions reveal your values.
138. • Your thought is the most powerful force in your universe. "Nothing is either good or bad but thinking makes it so." -Shakespeare.
139. • Be courageous! Whatever you dwell on expands.
140. • Work toward goals that cause you to feel a sense of mastery.
141. • Write a list of everything you have accomplished or have been recognized for in your life. Add to it whenever you think of something new. Read it when the going gets tough.
142. • Have a clear sense of purpose in life.
143. • Clarify your goals and focus on them
144. • Be a risk taker. Step outside your comfort zone. Try something new.
145. • Positive expectations are the single, most outwardly identifiable, characteristics all successful people possess.

146. • You can train yourself to think more positively by training yourself to choose what you pay attention to and what you say about it, both to yourself and others. "We know what we are but know not what we may be." -Shakespeare.

147. • Whatever you believe, picture in your mind, and think about most of the time, you eventually will bring into reality.

148. • Your self-image is the most dominant factor that affects everything you attempt to do.

149. • Nothing is more exciting than the realization that you can accomplish anything you really want that is consistent with your unique mix of natural talents and abilities.

150. • Remember, "Change your thoughts and you change your world." - Norman Vincent Peale.

WORTHY QUOTES

- It is not the place, nor the condition, but the mind alone that can make any one happy or miserable. - L Estrange.
- Beliefs have the power to create and the power to destroy.
- Nothing is more likely to help a person overcome or endure troubles than the consciousness of having a task in life. –Victor Frankl.
- When the student is ready, the teacher will appear. - Zen proverb.
- The ancestor to every action is a thought. -Emerson.
- Things do not change; we change. -Thoreau.
- Great men are those who see that thoughts rule the world. -Emerson.
- The greatest discovery of my generation is that human beings can alter their lives by altering their attitudes of mind. -William James.
- The only limits you have are the limits you believe. -Wayne Dyer.
- Anything we fail to reinforce will eventually dissipate. -Robbins.
- Patience is the companion of wisdom. -Augustine.
- The more he gives to others, the more he possesses of his own. -Lao-Tzu.
- Vision is the art of seeing things invisible. -Swift.
- Believing is seeing. -Dyer.
- We become what we envision. -Claude Bristol
- Our aspirations are our possibilities. -Robert Browning
- Success means living the life of the heart. -Frances Ford Coppola
- The size of your success is determined by the size of your belief. -Lucius Annaeus Seneca
- It is not hard to make decisions when you know what your values are. - Roy Disney
- Work is love made visible. -Kahil Gibran
- The man who really wants to do something finds a way; the other man finds an excuse. -E.C. McKenzie
- We are what we repeatedly do. Excellence, then, is not an act, but a habit. -Aristotle
- Only those who will risk going too far can possibly find out how far one can go. -T.S. Eliot
- Courage is rightly esteemed the first of human qualities because it is the quality which guarantees all others. -Winston Churchill

- I am a great believer in luck, and I find that the harder I work, the more I have of it. -Thomas Jefferson
- There are no wrong turns, only wrong thinking on the turns our life has taken. -Zen saying
- If we don't change our direction, we are likely to end up where we are headed. -Ancient Chinese Proverb
- Success is getting what you want. Happiness is wanting what you get.
  -Warren Buffett
- If he was to become himself, he must find a way to assemble the parts of his dreams into one whole. -George Eliot
- Lives based on having are less free than lives based on doing or being.
  -William James
- There is no security in life, only opportunity. -Mark Twain
- You miss 100 percent of the shots you never take. -Wayne Gretzky
- All adventures, especially into new territories, are scary. -Sally Ride.
- The people who get on in this world are the people who get up and look for the circumstances they want, and, if they can't find them, make them. -George Bernard Shaw
- If you think you're too small to make a difference, you've never been in bed with a mosquito. -Anita Roddick
- Live neither in the past nor in the future, but let each day's work absorb your entire energies, and satisfy your wildest ambition. - William Osler
- The great use of life is to spend it for something that will outlast it.
  - William James

THANKS FOR MAKING A DIFFERENCE!

Printed in the United States
By Bookmasters